MAGIC THROUGH SCIENCE

MAGIC THROUGH SCIENCE

By Robert Gardner

Illustrated with photographs and with drawings by Jeff Brown

DOUBLEDAY & COMPANY, INC.
GARDEN CITY, NEW YORK

ISBN 0-385-12437-6 Trade
      0-385-12438-4 Prebound
Library of Congress Catalog Card Number 77–76239

To Natalie

CONTENTS

MAGIC
THROUGH
SCIENCE

Before the Show Begins

Almost everyone enjoys a magic show. A good magician can provide an hour or two of exciting entertainment. Some people are so mystified by a magician's feats that they think he has superhuman powers. But, as any honest magician will tell you, he is just a normal human being. What he has learned is a way to make things *seem* to happen—things that could never really happen at all.

Most of the "magic" in this book is not the kind that magicians do. There is no sleight of hand, no palming, no hidden wire, no trap door. The "tricks" that you will learn are not really tricks at all. The "magic" that you will do is natural magic. It's just the way chemicals react or the behavior of objects that interact. Nature provides the mystery because natural events, reactions, and interactions are often as amazing, exciting, and mysterious as the tricks that magicians use to fool you.

Because these tricks are not based on deception, they are easier to do than a magician's magic. All you have to do is bring the proper ingredients together or put them in the right places. Nature does the rest.

It's fun to prepare and perform a science magic show, but it does require lots of practice if it is to be successful. If you don't like to stand before an audience, you can find enjoyment in *doing* many of the scenes in this book for an audience of one—yourself!

THE ACTS

This book is divided into eight acts. As in a play, each act contains a number of related scenes that you might include in your science magic show.

Each scene contains the following sections:

Action!: a description of the scene as the audience will see it.

Props and Prep: a list of the items needed to perform the scene as well as a description of any special preparations you must make before the performance.

Explanation: an explanation of why the action described takes place.

A few scene titles are followed by the words: "for a small audience." These scenes involve materials or observations that would not be visible to a large audience. A "small audience" means a dozen or fewer people.

PATTER AND ON-STAGE BEHAVIOR

Every successful magician has an appealing way of presenting his act. Through his words and actions he gets the attention of his audience and keeps their interest.

You will need some patter to go along with the action in many of the scenes you do. The author will suggest some words you might like to use for a few of the scenes. However, if you find it fun to invent the chatter you use in your act, you will probably want to write a script and develop a style of your own—a style that works for you.

Always respect your audience. Laugh with them but never at them. If something doesn't work, take it in stride and move on to the next scene. Science magic is quite different from other magic shows your audience may have seen. It might be a good idea to explain this to them at the start of your show. To help your audience to understand the difference between magic and science magic, you might like to do several scenes from Acts I and II before you begin your science magic. Acts I and II are a few of the tricks that magicians do.

REHEARSAL

A good magician practices each trick he uses in a show until he can do it perfectly, but he seldom repeats a trick before the same audience. Some people might figure out how he does it if they saw it twice. As a science magician, you should practice a lot too, but you can repeat your scenes if the audience wants you to because there is no deception involved.

You might like to practice with a friend, a brother, or a sister who could be your associate or assistant. Or you can get together with several people and present a show in which each of you does a few scenes.

Don't try to do a show until you have practiced and perfected every scene you plan to use. Try each scene before a small audience such as your family before you do it in front of a larger audience. If you have difficulty with a scene, don't use it. Replace it with one you perform well or present a shorter show. Remember—your audience will prefer a brief good show rather than a long poor one.

SOURCES FOR PROPS

Many of the chemicals you will need can be found in your kitchen, garage, basement, or bathroom cabinet. Some of the other chemicals may be purchased from a drugstore, hobby shop, or toy store. Chemistry sets will have some of the chemicals you need. You may be able to obtain chemicals from your school laboratory. Ask the science teacher for permission. If you explain what you need them for, he or she might even help you, just to see what happens, or encourage you to do a number of related scenes as a science project.

Glassware and most of the other materials you will use can be found in your home or school.

SAFETY

Some of the scenes you do may require using poisonous chemicals. Others can be performed only by using a burner flame. I have pointed out the specific dangers involved in doing certain scenes, but you should always observe the following general safety rules.

1. Wash your hands thoroughly after working with chemicals. Use lots of soap and water. Similarly, thoroughly wash and rinse all the glassware you use.

2. Do not touch your mouth with your fingers while working with chemicals.

3. Wear safety glasses when heating glassware or flammable substances.

4. Keep flames away from flammable objects such as papers, clothing, hair, curtains, etc.

5. Have a fire extinguisher nearby when you use a flame.

6. Have a large pail or waste basket three-quarters full of sand close at hand when you use a flame. Flaming objects can be dropped into the sand or the sand can be used to smother a fire.

7. Unless you work on a fire-resistant table, cover the table with a heat-proof mat when you work with flames or hot objects.

8. Keep all flames away from your audience.

9. Whenever you insert glass tubing into a rubber stopper or cork, lubricate the outer surface of the glass with a drop of glycerine. Always hold the tubing with your fingers close to the stopper or cork.

10. If you are not sure of what you are doing, consult an adult. Always ask your parent or guardian for permission be-

fore you use flames or chemicals or borrow items to use in your act.

Most of these rules are just common sense, but it is essential that you observe them. If you are careful and work safely, science magic is fun, but foolish or unsafe behavior could lead to an accident.

Act I

Magicians' Magic

A good magician is a clever and accomplished actor who does things that mystify his audience. Most of the "magic" that you will learn to do in this book will mystify your audience too, but it can all be explained on the basis of scientific principles.

Before you begin to practice and perfect your magic show or just try the scenes in this book for your own enjoyment, you might like to learn a few tricks that magicians do. Then you will have an idea of how magicians fool you. You might even like to try some of these tricks on other people.

Even though you know a magician uses tricks to make things *seem* to happen, you can still enjoy a good magic show. It's fun to see if you can figure out how he does each trick. Remember, these are magicians' tricks! A magician would do these only once with the same audience.

SCENE 1: PICK A CARD

Action! Shuffle a pack of cards and cut the deck into two piles. Ask someone to pick a card from one of the piles, look at it, and place it on top of the second pile. Then place the first pile on top of the second. Ask your subject to cut the cards once or twice. Now spread out the cards face up and pick the one your subject looked at.

Props and Prep

Deck of 52 cards

Explanation

When you pick up the first pile, you casually look at the bottom card. The card your subject picked will be just beneath this card. The chance that a cut will separate these two cards is only 1 in 52.

SCENE 2: ONE OF FOUR

Action! Deal a row of four cards face down. Ask someone to pick one card, look at it, show it to the audience, and replace it while you turn around. Mix the cards and put them in your pocket. Then pull out the card your subject chose. After showing the card to your audience, remove three more cards from your pocket and show them to your audience. All the cards are different.

Props and Prep

2 identical decks of pinochle cards

Select four identical cards and three other cards from the two decks. Put the three cards that are all different in your pocket.

Explanation

All four cards that you dealt were the same. They were taken from two identical pinochle decks. Place these cards in your pocket in front of the other three already there. Return one of them to your subject. The three other cards that you return are cards that you placed in your pocket before the scene.

SCENE 3: PICK A BUCK

Action! Collect a number of dollar bills from your audience. Ask one person from whom you are collecting a dollar to write down its serial number. Wad each bill into a ball and drop it into a hat. Shake the hat, place it on a table, turn your head away, reach into the hat, and pull out a bill. You have picked the bill for which the serial number was recorded.

Props and Prep

Hat
Small marble
Dollar bills
Paper
Pencil

Explanation

When you wad the bill for which the serial number has been recorded, you place a small marble in the center of the bill. When you reach into the hat, you pick the heaviest bill. Squeeze the marble from the bill before you remove it from the hat and hand it to the subject who recorded the serial number.

This trick requires you to palm a small marble (hide it in your hand) before wadding a dollar bill around it.

SCENE 4: GUESS AGAIN

Action! Place four white poker chips on a table. Take a pencil and mark a small X on one chip. Turn the chip over and move the chips around. Ask someone who has been watching carefully to pick the marked chip. His guess is wrong. Turn up another chip. The X is on it.

Props and Prep

4 white poker chips
Pencil

Mark an X on the bottom of three chips before the scene begins.

Explanation

When you turn over the chip you marked in front of your audience, you draw your moist thumb across it, thus erasing the X. But an X has been marked on the underside of the three other chips before the scene started. So the one you choose will have an X on it.

SCENE 5: THE BURNED INITIAL

Action! Ask someone to write the initial of his first name on a small sheet of paper. Then light a large wooden kitchen match and burn the piece of paper in a metal container or sink. As the paper burns, tell the audience that the initial has been transferred to the match. The initial that was written on the paper can be seen on the burned match head.

Props and Prep

Kitchen match
Pin
Paper
Pencil

Use a pin to scratch an initial on the match head before the show.

Explanation

The initial you scratch into the match head is that of someone you know will be in the audience. Ask him or her to write on the paper. The initial will be visible after the match head has burned. Notice! You did not mention what would happen to the initial until *after* you lit the match. If you had, someone might have asked to inspect the match head.

SCENE 6: YOUR BIRTHDAY

Action! Tell someone you will be able to determine his or her birthday if he or she will do some arithmetic. Give him or her a pencil and a piece of paper. Then tell that person to do the following:

"Take the number of the month that you were born (January is 1, February is 2, March is 3, etc.).

"Multiply that number by 5.

"Add 4.

"Multiply the sum by 10.

"Add 9.

"Multiply the sum by 2.

"Add the number of the day of the month on which you were born."

Then ask, "What number do you have?"

After the reply, tell the person his or her birthday!

Explanation

You simply subtract 98 from the final number the subject gave you (or subtract 100 and add 2). The last one or two digits of this remainder are the day of the month he was born. The first one or two digits give you the month.

All the arithmetic you ask the person to do is just a way of getting him to multiply the month in which he was born by 100 to which he adds 98. You subtract the 98 after he adds the day of month he was born. This leaves him with a number that is 100 times the number of his birth month plus the day on which he was born.

Try this with your own birthday. As an example, suppose you were born on October 10 (10/10):

$$10 \times 5 = 50$$
$$50 + 4 = 54$$
Subject's arithmetic $\quad 54 \times 10 = 540$
$$540 + 9 = 549$$
$$549 \times 2 = 1,098$$
$$1098 + 10 = 1,108$$

Your arithmetic $\quad 1108 - 98 = 1,010$
$$10/10 = \text{October } 10$$

Or suppose it was February 8 (2/8):

Subject's arithmetic	$2\times 5= 10$ $10+ 4= 14$ $14\times 10=140$ $140+ 9=149$ $149\times 2=298$ $298+ 8=306$
Your arithmetic	$306-98=208$ $2/08=$February 8

SCENE 7: MAGNIFICENT MEMORY

Action! Tell your audience that you have memorized the names in a telephone book. Ask for two volunteers to help you demonstrate your memory. Give one of them a pad of paper and a pencil. Hand the telephone book to the other one. Ask the first to write down a three digit number such that all three digits are different (534, for example). Tell him to reverse the order of the digits (534 will become 435) and subtract the smaller number from the larger. (534—435=99). Ask him if the remainder has three digits. [If it doesn't, tell him to add a zero (99 will become 990)]. Now tell him to reverse the order of the digits in this remainder (990 will become 099) and add it to the remainder itself (990+099=1,089).

Ask the volunteer to tell you the last *two* digits of the number he has obtained. Tell the person holding the telephone book to turn to that page (89). Now ask for the first two digits (10). Ask your second volunteer to count down the page to the tenth telephone number on the page. Finally, ask the first volunteer to write the telephone number in large print on a sheet of paper and show it to the audience, while concealing it from you.

Pretend to concentrate very hard for several moments, and then announce the phone number and the name of the owner.

The audience is amazed to find that the number is the same

as the one being held before them. The volunteer confirms the fact that the name is correct as well.

Props and Prep

Telephone book
Pencil
Paper

Before the show begins, memorize the tenth name and number on page 89 of the telephone book.

Explanation

If the first volunteer does his arithmetic correctly, the number he gets will always be 1,089. Try it a few times and you'll see that it always works!

SCENE 8: A MYSTERIOUS MARBLE (for a small audience)

Action! Place three small empty matchboxes (not matchbooks) on a table. Tell the audience that there is a small marble in one of the boxes. You prove it by shaking one of the boxes. It rattles. When you shake the other two boxes, there is no noise.

Then mix the boxes by moving them around and ask a member of the audience to pick the box that has the marble. When he shakes the box, it is empty. You say, "I thought it was in this one!" You shake another box and, sure enough, it rattles!

Mix the boxes again and let someone else try to choose the box with the marble. Again, the volunteer is wrong, but you find the correct box immediately.

Props and Prep

4 small empty matchboxes
Tape
Small marble

Before the show you place a small marble in one of the boxes and seal all four boxes with tape. Fasten the box with the marble to your right forearm with tape or a rubber band. Put on a coat so the sleeve hides the box.

Explanation

All the boxes the audience picks are empty. They can't win! When you pick up the "right" box, you use your right hand. The box taped to your right arm rattles but the audience thinks it is the box in your hand. When you want to show another box is empty, you use your left hand.

Act II

ESP

Some people believe that one person can communicate with another without a word being said or written. They think that messages or feelings can be sent from one brain to another by some mysterious process called "telepathy." Since this form of communication does not involve any of the normal senses (sight, hearing, touch, smell, taste), it is a type of extra-sensory perception, or ESP for short. There are people who believe that ESP exists. There are others who doubt that telepathy, or ESP, is possible. They believe that reports of ESP can be explained by the laws of probability.

The scenes in this act can be used to test for ESP. Perhaps you will find people who really have the ability to communicate through telepathy. These scenes may also be used to demonstrate how people can be made to believe in ESP when, in fact, they are being tricked.

SCENE 1: NAME THE OBJECT

Action! Ask for a volunteer who believes he or she possesses ESP. This person is sent from the room. When the person comes back, he is asked to identify an object chosen by the audience during his absence.

After the person returns, ask someone with whom the subject thinks he can communicate through ESP to point to a number of objects one at a time. Each time the subject is asked, "Is this it?"

Generally, the person will be unable to identify the item that was chosen.

After several people have tried their own ESP skills, select someone you say will be able to pick the correct object every time when *you* ask the questions.

Suggest to the audience that some people can communicate through ESP while others cannot. When you point to the objects, the person you selected is always able to choose the correct item. When someone else points out the objects, the same person seldom picks the correct item.

Props and Prep

Room with a number of objects

Before the show, establish a set of signals with one member of the audience.

Explanation

Unless you discover someone who truly possesses ESP, the only person who will succeed consistently is the one with whom you have established signals. As an example, the signal might be that the correct item will be the one you point to immediately after you point to a *black* object.

After a few trials, someone in the audience may want you to point to the chosen object first. This requires that additional signals be established ahead of time, such as indicating normal procedure by pointing to the first object with your right hand or indicating that the chosen object is the first one and that a color code is impossible, by pointing with your left hand.

If your audience suspects signals, you must have extra signals that would enable you to change the indicator color during the scene.

SCENE 2: NAME THE CARD (for a small audience)

Action! Place nine playing cards face up on a table in three rows of three cards as shown in the photograph.

A person who thinks he or she may possess ESP is sent from the room. The audience selects one of the cards for the person to identify. When the person returns, point to the cards one at a time. Each time you ask, "Is this the card?"

Usually, the person will respond, after you have pointed to two or three cards, "Yes, that's the one!"

After several people have tried unsuccessfully, a person is found who can pick the correct card *every* time you do the pointing.

Props and Prep

Deck of 52 cards

Establish a set of signals with one member of the audience before the show begins.

Explanation

Unless you discover someone who truly possesses ESP, the only person who will succeed consistently is the one with whom you have established signals.

The signal is given when you point to the first card. The nine cards can be thought of as nine positions on a rectangle: one in each of the *four* corners, one along each of the *four* edges, and one in the *center*. When you point to the *first* card, you are careful to place your fingertip at a point on the card that indicates the chosen card. For instance, if you place your finger on the center of any one of the nine cards, it means that the card in the center of the nine-card rectangle is the one the audience picked. After you give the signal with your first pointing, your partner knows which card was chosen so you can place your finger anywhere on the next cards you point to.

In the picture above, the fingertip position indicates that the card picked by the audience was the three of hearts. If the fingertip were on the "K" on the outside corner of the card, it would indicate that the card being touched, the king of diamonds, was the one chosen.

If your audience suspects signals, they will ask you to point to the chosen card first. Your partner must be ready to pick the first card if that's what your signal indicates.

SCENE 3: MUSCLE ESP

Action! Announce that you and your assistant have a way of communicating through ESP, but that muscle action and an antenna are needed if the brain waves are to be transmitted from one to the other with enough strength to be received.

Your partner leaves the room. A member of the audience chooses some object in the room for your assistant to identify.

After your partner returns, you talk, draw strange symbols on the floor with a stick or broom handle (your antenna), and tap the floor with the stick.

For example, suppose someone picked a red chair for your partner to identify.

Your partner returns and you say, "*R*eady."

You then draw a symbol with the stick, tap the floor *twice,* and say, "*D*on't be tense!"

You draw another symbol as you say, "*C*an you follow me? . . . *H*ang on!"

You tap the floor *once,* draw a symbol, tap the floor *three* times, and say, "*R*eady to name the object?"

Your partner points to the red chair!

Props and Prep

Room with a number of objects
Broom or sticklike object

Establish a set of signals with your assistant ahead of time.

Explanation

The symbols are merely decoys. You communicate through speech and by taps with the stick.

In the example, you signaled "RED CHAIR."

The *first* letter in each sentence you speak indicates a consonant. In the example above, you said, "*R*eady?" indicating the first letter was "R." To indicate that the second letter was

"E," you tapped twice. Vowels are communicated by the number of taps:

> 1 tap indicates A
> 2 taps indicate E
> 3 taps indicate I
> 4 taps indicate O
> 5 taps indicate U

Note the first letter (underlined) of each spoken sentence in the sample. Also record the vowels from the number of taps (also underlined). You will see that all together they spell "RED CHAIR."

If there was only one chair in the room, "RED" would not be needed. You might begin by saying, "*C*ome on now, let's begin!"

If there was more than one red chair, your partner might say, "I know it's a red chair but I don't know which one."

You could supply more information about the chair using the same technique.

SCENE 4: WHICH HAND HOLDS THE COIN?

Action! Announce that you are going to see if someone can communicate a simple message to you through ESP. Ask for a volunteer. Hand him a coin. Turn away and tell him to put the coin in either of his hands. Then say, "Place the fist that's holding the coin against your forehead. Concentrate on the coin. Wipe out all other thoughts. Concentrate . . . concentrate . . . concentrate."

After about half a minute, say to him, "Hold out *both* fists but don't let me see the coin."

You turn quickly and pick the hand that holds the coin.

Props and Prep

Coin

Explanation

When someone holds a hand up, the blood supply in that hand decreases. Look for the hand that is paler and with the less noticeable veins. It will be the one that he used to hold the coin to his forehead.

Act III

Magic over Mind

In this act most of the scenes require the audience to partici-
pate and to use materials if they are to see the "magic." With
the exception of the first and last scenes, materials have to be
distributed to the audience. Because it takes time to distribute
materials, Scenes 2, 3, 4, and 5 should be performed only
with a small audience.

SCENE 1: A SUSPENDED SAUSAGE

Action! Tell the members of the audience to focus their
eyes on a distant object while they bring the tips of their index
fingers together at a point about 10 to 20 centimeters (4 to 8
inches) in front of their eyes. Now tell them to move their
finger tips slightly apart. They will see a "sausage" suspended
in midair that seems to defy gravity.

Props and Prep

None are needed

Explanation

Human eyes are several centimeters apart. Because of this,
the image formed on one retina is slightly different from the

image on the other retina. Light from the object being viewed strikes each eye at slightly different angles.

When you look at something close by, you turn your eyes in. The two images fall on very nearly the same region (the center) of each retina. The impulses that travel to the brain give us a fused view of the object. The central part of the image is the same in both eyes, but the right eye sees farther around the right side of the object and the left eye farther around the left side. The fusion of these images in the brain gives us a three-dimensional view.

When you look at something far away, your eyes are nearly parallel, looking straight ahead. A nearby object is generally ignored. If you pay attention to a nearby object while your eyes focus on a distant object, you will see two images of that object. As you can see in the drawing, the image of the nearby object will fall on the right side of your right retina and on the left side of your left retina. The brain is unable to "fuse" these images, so you perceive two views at the same time.

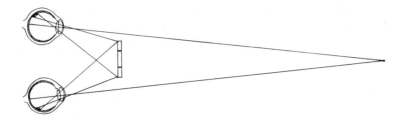

If you focus your eyes on a nearby object, will you see double images of distant objects?

Do you see now why people see a "sausage"? If not, try this! With the "sausage" in view, close first one eye and then the other. You will see only one image when one eye is closed. Notice how the image seen by your right eye differs in position from the one you see with your left eye.

SCENE 2: A HOLE IN THE HAND

Action! Give each member of your audience a sheet of paper and tell them to roll it into a cylinder about 3 centimeters (1¼ inches) in diameter. Instruct them to look through the tubes with their right eyes as they focus both eyes on some distant object. Then tell them to hold their left hands at arm's length and slowly move it from left to right toward the tubes. A hole will seem to appear in their left hands.

Props and Prep

Sheets of paper

Explanation

As explained in Scene 1, each of your eyes receives a different image on the center of the retina. In this example, the distant image falls on the center of your right retina. The image of the hand falls on the center of your left retina. The tube blocks out light coming from your hand to your right eye. Instead of seeing a double image of your hand, you see the hand with the image seen through the tube superimposed on it. It is perceived as if there were a hole in the left hand.

SCENE 3: A DISAPPEARING LETTER (for a small audience)

Action! Ask each member of the audience to draw the letter *X* on a small card. Tell them all to close their left eyes and focus their right eyes on a distant object. Have them hold the cards in their right hands at arm's length and slightly to the right of their open eyes. Instruct them to move the cards slowly toward their right eyes. At some point the Xs will disappear. They can be made to reappear by moving the cards either forward or backward.

Props and Prep

    File cards
    Pencils (or premark each card with an X)

Explanation

There is a small area near the center of the retina where the optic nerve enters the eye. There are no light-sensitive cells there. Images falling in this area, called the "blind spot," cannot be seen. When the image of the X formed by the eye's lens falls on this spot, the X seems to disappear. (Try a big X! Only part of the X will disappear. Why?)

SCENE 4: AN UPSIDE-DOWN SHADOW (for a small audience)

Action! Hand each person in the audience a file card and a pin. Tell them to make pinholes in the center of the cards. Then tell them to hold their cards about 30 centimeters (1 foot) in front of one eye and look through the pinhole toward a bright, uniform surface. The sky or a well-illuminated light-colored wall are both good. As they look through the pinholes, tell them to *very carefully* move the *head* of their pins up and down in front of and very close to the pupils of the eyes they are using. They will see shadows. But what else do they notice? If they look closely, they will see the shadows move down when the pinheads move *up!* When the pinheads move down, the shadows move *up!*

Props and Prep

    File cards
    Common pins

To save time, you might prepunch a pinhole in each card.

Explanation

When you look at an object, the lens of your eye bends the light rays and produces an *upside-down* image of the object on your retina (see Act V, Scene 7). You have learned through experience to interpret these images as if they were right side up. But if the object is very close to the eye, the lens cannot bend light enough to produce an image. The pinhead in this example is too close for the lens to make an image of it, but the narrow beam of light coming through the pinhole casts the shadow of the pinhead on your retina. As the upright pinhead moves up across your pupil, its shadow moves up across your retina. But you have learned to reverse the images (or shadows) cast on your retina. Therefore, your brain interprets the nerve impulses it receives as an upside-down pinhead moving downward.

SCENE 5: YOU CAN PUT A FISH IN WATER BUT YOU CAN'T MAKE HIM DRINK (for a small audience)

Action! Show your audience a white card that has a fish drawn on one side and a fish bowl on the other. Place the card in a slot cut in a wooden dowel. When you rotate the card swiftly by spinning the dowel back and forth between your hands, the fish appears to be in the bowl.

Props and Prep

White card (about 12×20 cm [5×8 in.])
Wooden dowel, slit in one end

To cut the slit in the dowel, use a fine saw. If the card doesn't fit tightly, fold the edge of the card or wedge small pieces of paper or cardboard into the slit to fill up the space. Alternatively, you can cut the card so it has a tab at the bottom. Then tape this tab to the wooden dowel.

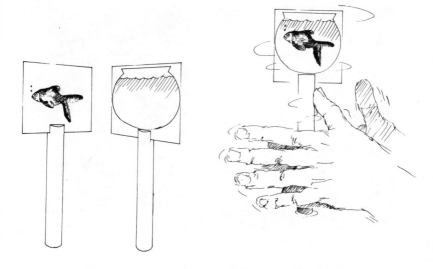

Explanation

Images formed on your retina do not disappear immediately. They persist for about $\frac{1}{15}$ second. Because of this, we see a motion picture as a continuous flow of motion not a series of still pictures. Actually, when you watch a movie, you see twenty-four separate pictures each second. You aren't aware of this because the time between pictures ($\frac{1}{24}$ second) is less than the time an image remains on your retina. As one image fades, it is replaced by another.

By spinning the card fast, the image of the fish still remains on your retina when the image of the bowl is formed there.

SCENE 6: DRAG A CIRCLE

Action! Show the audience a large card that is half black and half white. The black-white intersection lies underneath the vertical diameter of a gray paper ring glued to the center of the card.

When a stick or ruler is laid along the vertical diameter of

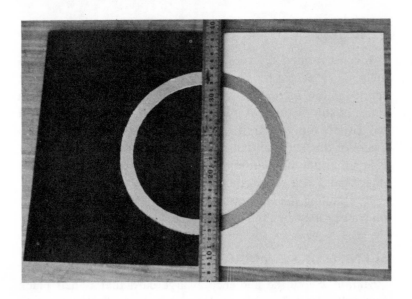

the ring, the half of the ring that lies on the white background suddenly appears much darker than the half that lies on the black background, as you can see in the picture.

Even more startling is the fact that you can "drag" either

the light or dark half of the ring into the other half of the card by slowly moving the stick to the right or left along the paper.

Props and Prep

Sheet of black paper
Sheet of white paper
Sheet of gray paper
Sheet of cardboard (rectangular)
Stick or ruler
Glue

Tape the black and white sheets together to form a rectangle about 40×30 centimeters (15 by 12 inches). Mount this rectangle on the cardboard.

Cut a ring from the gray paper. It should be about 2 centimeters (¾ inches) wide, with a diameter of about 20 centimeters (8 inches). Glue the ring to the cardboard so its diameter lies along the black-white intersection as shown in the pictures.

Explanation

The messages about brightness that your eyes send to your brain seem to be interpreted in a relative way. A light bulb that appears very bright at night might very well go unnoticed on a sunny day.

When you place the stick along the diameter of the gray ring, you immediately notice the contrast between gray on white and gray on black. Small involuntary movements of your eyes probably cause light from the gray ring to fall on light-sensitive cells in your eyes that have just been stimulated by the more intense light from the white background. These cells are "tired" from the intense light they've been receiving and so are less responsive than they were earlier. The brain interprets this to mean that the gray is darker than it really is. On the black background the gray looks lighter because the lack of light from the black enables the retinal cells to rest and become very sensitive. These rested cells send more impulses to your brain, which interprets that as a brighter gray than normal.

The reason you can "drag" half of the circle into the other half is difficult to explain. It is certainly a psychological effect that probably has to do with your realization or expectation of something uniform in shape or color to maintain that uniformity.

Act IV

Magic with Kitchen Chemicals

The scenes in this act make use of items and chemicals that you can find in your kitchen, bathroom cabinet, or basement.

SCENE 1: THE MAGIC MESSAGE

Action! Show your audience a plain white file card. You hold the card above a candle or alcohol-burner flame and move it back and forth being careful not to scorch it. After a minute or so, words appear on the card. They might say "MAGIC," "HOT PRINT," "WELCOME," or whatever you like.

After the audience has seen the message, place the card on a table and blot it gently (don't rub) with a folded facial tissue that you dipped in a liquid.

Show the audience that the message has disappeared!

Blot the card with a *dry* tissue and move it over the flame again. The message reappears, fainter but readable.

Props and Prep

Lemon juice
Liquid household bleach **(poisonous)**
White file card
Facial tissue or toilet paper

Toothpick
Matches
Candle or alcohol burner
Holder for candle

Before the show, write the message on the card with lemon juice. A toothpick can serve as a pen.

The liquid used to blot away the message is household bleach. **Liquid bleach is poisonous. Keep it away from your eyes and mouth!**

Explanation

Lemon juice contains citric acid. When dry, citric acid is a white powder. If the acid is heated, it decomposes into carbon and other colored substances. The bleach converts these colored substances into colorless ones. The second heating again decomposes colorless substances into dark products.

You might like to heat some citric acid crystals in a test tube. What happens? Keep heating until you see a color change!

SCENE 2: GENIE IN A BOTTLE

Action! "Let's see if the spirits are with us tonight," you say to the audience. Point to a narrow-necked bottle filled with a dark liquid and say, "A genie lives in this bottle. Let's see if we can get him to come out!"

Cover the opening of a second narrow-necked, water-filled bottle with a small piece of paper towel. Turn the bottle over; the water does not come out. (Do you know why?) Place this inverted bottle on top of the one filled with a dark liquid and carefully pull the piece of towel from between the mouths of the bottles. A dark wispy "genie" emerges and rises into the upper bottle.

Props and Prep

> 2 clear narrow-neck bottles
> Black ink
> Hot water
> Cold water
> Paper towel

Just before the scene begins, fill one bottle to the very top with *hot* water and enough black ink to make the liquid very dark. Completely fill the second bottle, the one that is to be inverted, with cold water.

Explanation

The cold water does not come out of the inverted bottle because the air pressure on the bottom of the piece of towel is greater than the pressure of the water above the towel. In fact, it would take the pressure of a column of water 10 meters (33 feet) tall to equal the pressure of the air at sea level.

The inky water rises into the upper bottle because hot water is less dense than cold water. The cold water in the upper bottle falls downward as the warmer inky water rises.

You can check this more directly by inserting an eyedropper full of warm inky water down into the center of a glass of cold water and *slowly* squeezing out its contents. You will see the dark water rise to the surface of the denser cold water.

SCENE 3: DISAPPEARING INK

Action! Add a drop or two of black ink to some water in a clear glass tumbler or beaker and stir to mix. A colorless "magic" liquid is added to the dark water. After stirring for a minute or so, the dark liquid becomes clear.

Props and Prep

> Black ink
> Clear glass tumbler or beaker
> Liquid household bleach **(poisonous)**
> Stirring instrument
> Eyedropper (optional)
> Water

You'll want to practice this scene a few times to get the proper quantities.

Bleach is poisonous. Keep it away from your eyes and mouth. Be sure to rinse all glasses thoroughly after using.

Explanation

The "magic" liquid added to the ink solution is bleach. The bleach releases oxygen that combines with the colored chemicals in the ink to form colorless substances. Stirring insures thorough contact between bleach and ink.

SCENE 4: CIDER TO INK

Action! Point to a glass filled with a straw-colored liquid and announce that you will change the "cider" to "ink." Pour the liquid into another glass that contains a "magic" white powder. After the liquid has been poured back and forth from one glass to the other several times, the liquid becomes dark blue.

Props and Prep

> 2 clear glass tumblers or beakers
> Teaspoon
> Tincture of iodine **(poisonous)**
> Cornstarch or flour
> Water

Add ¼ teaspoon of cornstarch to an empty glass. If cornstarch is not available, you may substitute flour.

Add ¼ teaspoon of tincture of iodine to a glass of water to make the "cider." **Iodine is poisonous. Keep it away from your eyes and mouth. Be sure to rinse glasses and spoon thoroughly after use.**

Explanation

When starch and an iodine solution are mixed, a complex substance with a very dark blue color is produced. In fact, the addition of a dilute iodine solution is used as a test for the presence of starch. You might like to try this test by adding a few drops of a dilute iodine solution to small pieces of starchy foods such as bread, cake, and raw potatoes, as well as to pure starch and flour. Of course, these substances should not be eaten after testing because **iodine is poisonous.**

SCENE 5: GRAPE TO MINT TO GRAPE

Action! Pour some unsweetened grape juice into a clear glass tumbler and add water to make the color much less intense (about one part juice to nine parts water; you need not measure—just make an estimate).

Tell the audience to watch closely as you change the grape juice to liquid mint. Pour the juice into a second tumbler and the juice changes from a light red color to a deep green!

Then tell them that you will change the liquid mint back to grape juice. Pour the green liquid into a third glass and it becomes a light red color again!

Repeat the procedure a second time with three more tumblers using a larger volume of diluted juice. As you prepare to pour the liquid into the last glass, mention that it is only possible to convert a limited amount of mint juice back into grape juice because the converting "spirit" in the glass tires quickly. As you begin to pour the green solution it appears to be converted to grape juice, but as you add more of the solution, the liquid becomes green again! The "spirit" has tired.

Props and Prep

Grape juice (no sugar added)
Water
Household ammonia **(poisonous)**
White vinegar
6 clear glass tumblers, jars, or beakers

Before the first part of the scene, add several drops of ammonia to the second glass. Add a milliliter or two of vinegar to the third glass. Use enough vinegar to change all the green liquid back to red. You'll have to practice this scene several times.

In the second part of the scene, you must be sure that you do *not* have enough vinegar to change all the green solution back to red. Use about 2 milliliters of ammonia in the second glass and 1 milliliter of vinegar in the third. **Be careful using the ammonia!**

Explanation

Grape juice is what is called an "indicator." It behaves something like litmus paper. When litmus paper is placed in an acid, it turns red. In a base, it turns blue. Grape juice turns red in acid and green in a base. Since household ammonia is a basic solution, the grape juice turns green when it is added to the ammonia in the second glass.

Vinegar is a dilute solution of acetic acid. When the green-colored basic solution is added to the acid in the third glass, the acid turns the solution back to a red color.

In the second part of the scene, all the acid is used up before it can neutralize the base. Remember, there was more ammonia in the second glass than vinegar in the third. Of course, if you want to, you can add more vinegar to the final green solution and change it to red.

From what you've seen, would you guess that grape juice is slightly acid, slightly basic, or neutral? If you have some litmus paper, you can check up on your prediction. You should also use a piece of white paper dipped in grape juice for comparison. Why?

SCENE 6: A BOTTLE GUN

Action! Announce that you have invented a bottle gun that fires cork "bullets." Quickly pour 30 milliliters (1 ounce) of liquid into a soda bottle. As soon as the liquid has been poured, push a cork firmly into the mouth of the bottle. Standing back from the bottle, shout, "Ready . . . aim . . . fire!"

As you say "Fire!" there is a loud pop and the cork flies out of the bottle and slams against the ceiling.

Props and Prep

Soda bottle
Baking soda
Vinegar
Cork to fit mouth of bottle

Be sure the bottle is not cracked; to be extra safe, wrap tape around the bottle.

The bottom of the bottle should be covered with baking soda before the show. To pour this powder through the narrow mouth of the bottle, roll a piece of paper into a funnel shape and place it in the mouth of the bottle. Let the powder slide down the funnel into the bottle.

The liquid added to the bottle is vinegar, which acts on the baking soda to produce a gas. Cork it quickly so that very little gas escapes.

Be sure the bottle is "aimed" upward away from the audience because the cork is shot out of the bottle at a very high speed.

Explanation

The acetic acid in the vinegar reacts with baking soda, which is sodium bicarbonate, to form carbon dioxide gas. As more gas is produced in the closed bottle, the pressure inside the bottle increases. (This is just what happens when you pump air into a tire.) When the upward force on the cork becomes greater than the friction holding it, the cork loosens and is driven upward at a very high speed.

It's interesting to watch—**from a distance**—the reaction in the bottle after the cork is inserted. The rate of fizzing decreases as the pressure increases, illustrating a very basic chemical principle: in a chemical reaction that reaches equilibrium, an increase in the concentration of the products (carbon dioxide in this case) decreases the rate of the reaction that produces the products.

SCENE 7: BOTTLED ANTI-FIRE

Action! Light a candle and announce that you will extinguish it by making an "anti-fire spirit." Slowly pour 30 milliliters (1 ounce) of liquid into a white powder that covers the bottom of a wide-mouth bottle. The mixture fizzes, producing a lot of frothy bubbles. When the fizzing decreases, tip the bottle and pour the "anti-fire spirit," but not the liquid onto the candle flame. The flame goes out!

Props and Prep

Wide-mouth bottle (about 500 ml [1 pt])
Baking soda
Vinegar
Candle
Holder for candle
Matches

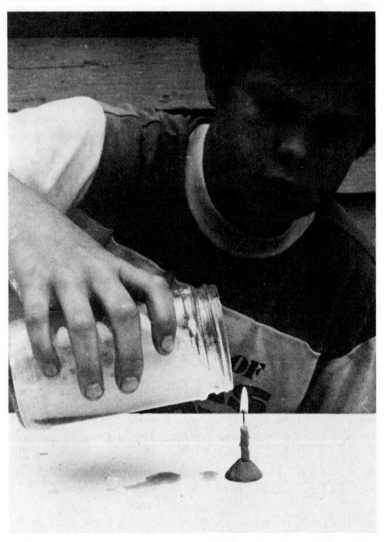

Cover the bottom of the wide-mouth bottle with a table-spoon of baking soda before the show. The liquid added to the powder is vinegar. When pouring the gas, be careful not to tip the bottle so far that liquid flows out the jar.

Explanation

When the acetic acid in vinegar reacts with the baking soda (sodium bicarbonate), carbon dioxide gas is produced. (You can also get carbon dioxide by dropping Alka-Seltzer tablets into a little water.) Since carbon dioxide is denser than air, it remains in the bottle when the bottle is upright. For the same reason, it flows down over the flame when you tip the bottle on one side.

Carbon dioxide is used in many fire extinguishers, since it does not burn or support combustion. Being so dense, it sinks onto a fire, displacing the less dense air so that the fire goes out.

SCENE 8: DANCING SPHERES

Action! Drop several moth balls into a tall, liquid-filled glass or jar. The moth balls sink, then rise, twist, and turn, only to sink again. This sink-and-rise pattern goes on for hours.

Props and Prep

Moth balls
Glass jar or tall beaker
Vinegar
Water
Baking soda

Just before you start this scene, cover the bottom of the glass with about a tablespoon of baking soda. Add water slowly down the side of the glass so as to disturb the powder as little as possible until the glass is nearly full. Slowly add about 30 milliliters (1 ounce) of vinegar to the water. The baking soda that has dissolved in the water will fizz as the vinegar is added. Add another 30 milliliters of vinegar, to react slowly with the undissolved baking soda on the bottom of the jar. Now you are ready to add moth balls.

If the "dance" becomes too slow, add a little more vinegar to increase the tempo.

Explanation

Moth balls are slightly more dense than plain water and sink when dropped into it.

The acetic acid in the vinegar reacts with the baking soda (sodium bicarbonate) to form carbon dioxide gas. Bubbles of this gas adhere to the surface of the moth balls. When the combined density of the moth balls and the attached bubbles becomes less than the density of vinegar and water, the moth balls ascend. At the surface of the liquid the bubbles are slowly released to the air. This process is not uniform. There may be more bubbles on one side of a moth ball than elsewhere. This causes the moth ball to turn or "dance" as its lighter side moves upward. After it loses a lot of bubbles, the density of the moth ball becomes greater than the density of water and it sinks again. So the process repeats itself.

SCENE 9: BOUNCING RAISINS

Action! Pour a clear carbonated beverage into a tall glass. Then add some quartered raisins. The raisin pieces sink, but soon rise to the surface, spin, turn, and then fall again. This process is repeated over and over again.

Props and Prep

Tall clear tumbler, jar, or beaker
Any light-colored carbonated beverage (e.g., ginger ale)
Raisins (cut into quarters)

Explanation

See explanation for Scene 8

SCENE 10: A FIREPROOF HANDKERCHIEF

Action! Take a clean white handkerchief and dip it into liquid and squeeze out the excess liquid with one hand. **Then pick up the handkerchief with a pair of long-handled metal forceps** and ignite it with your other hand. After the audience sees that the cloth is fully aflame, drop it into an empty *metal* wastebasket or a sink. Tell the audience not to worry about the handkerchief because you can reconstruct it from the ashes. You then pull the handkerchief from the receptacle.

If someone thinks it is a different handkerchief, invite him to look for the remains of the original in the wastebasket. He won't be able to find any.

Props and Prep

Glass or beaker
Mixture of half alcohol and half water
Matches
Cloth handkerchief
Metal wastebasket or suitable fireproof receptacle
Long-handled metal forceps

To avoid extensive flaming, **be sure to squeeze out the excess liquid from the handkerchief.** When you grasp the handkerchief with metal forceps, **hold it well away from your body or any flammable objects while it burns!**

Do not perform this scene if there is any danger that the fire may ignite other objects. It is best to practice this outdoors when there is no wind.

Explanation

When the handkerchief is ignited, only the alcohol portion of the liquid will burn. The non-flammable water remains in the cloth and keeps it from burning. (If pure alcohol were used, the high temperature from the burning process would ignite the handkerchief as well.)

SCENE 11: SINK OR FLOAT

Action! Place two clean plastic berry boxes on the surface of a large pan of water. Both boxes float. Then push them through the surface and they both sink, indicating that they are more dense than water. Shake the water from one box and place it back on the water. It floats as before. Remove this box and shake the water from the second box. Then announce that this box will not float if you touch it with a magic fluid. Rub a drop of liquid over the bottom of the box and place it gently on the water. It sinks as you predicted it would! Place the first box on the water now, and it too sinks!

Props and Prep

2 plastic berry boxes
Large container of clear water
Liquid detergent

The liquid which you rub on the bottom of the second box is liquid detergent.

Explanation

The boxes float because water has a high surface tension. The molecules of water on the surface are strongly attracted to one another and to the molecules below surface. This causes the water surface to hold together very well. It behaves as though it were like skin. You can see how the boxes dent this "skin" if you look carefully at the water surface between the cross pieces in the floating box.

The second box doesn't float when you put it back in the water because there is detergent on the bottom of the box. When detergent dissolves in water, it reduces the surface tension because it gets between the water molecules and reduces their attraction for one another. The weakened "skin" is easily broken by the weight of the box.

SCENE 12: A PAPER PERCOLATOR

Action! With a pair of long-handled metal forceps pick up a paper cup that contains about 30 milliliters (1 ounce) of water. Hold the cup over an alcohol or gas flame. Soon the water begins to boil, but the cup, even though made of paper, is only scorched. It does not burn.

Props and Prep

    Alcohol or gas burner
    Matches
    Small paper cup
    Water
    Forceps

Be very careful with fire. Do not do this or other scenes that involve flames if there is any danger of the fire spreading.

Keep hair, clothing, and other flammable objects away from the flame.

Explanation

The paper of the cup is thin enough to transfer the heat from the flame to the water. The heat then is used to warm and boil the water, not to burn the paper. The water temperature never rises above $100°C$ ($212°F$), its boiling point. This is well below the kindling temperature of paper.

SCENE 13: A JUMPING FLAME (for a small audience)

Action! Light a candle. After it has burned long enough for a full pool of melted wax to form around the wick, light a match. Then blow out the candle and quickly bring the burning match to a position 5 to 10 centimeters (2 to 4 inches) above the wick. The flame "jumps" from the match to the wick! The candle is burning again.

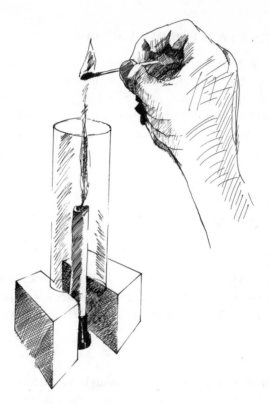

Next, place a clear lamp chimney or cylinder over the burning candle. (The chimney top should be 5 to 10 centimeters [2 to 4 inches] higher than the wick of the candle.) Again, blow out the candle and bring a burning match to the chimney top. A small blue flame moves down inside the chimney and settles on the wick. The candle is burning once more!

Props and Prep

Candle (about 2 to 3 cm [¾ to 1¼ in.] in diameter)
Holder for candle
Matches
Glass or plastic chimney or cylinder (slightly larger in diameter than the candle)

Practice this scene ahead of time. When you blow out the flame, look for a smoke stream rising from the candle and bring the match near it. In the second part, check a few times to be sure the chimney top is the right height above the candle. If the distance from chimney top to candle wick is too great, the blue flame will not travel down to the wick. The chimney makes the scene more dramatic because the flame can easily be seen moving 5 to 10 centimeters (2 to 4 inches) to the wick.

Be careful with candles and matches! Keep flames away from hair, clothing, and flammable objects!

Explanation

When the wick of a candle is ignited, its heat melts some of the candle wax. The liquid wax ascends the wick through the small spaces between the fibers just as water will rise in a paper towel. As the liquid wax gets closer to the flame, its temperature rises and it changes to a gas and burns.

(As you probably know, larger candles do not necessarily produce larger flames. The size of the flame is related to the wick size. To get a large flame, a thick wick with lots of fibers is necessary. This allows more wax vapor to get to the flame each second thereby providing more "fuel" for burning.)

After you blow out the candle in this scene, a trail of whitish wax vapor rises from the wick. This vapor is flammable. If you ignite it, the flame will follow the vapor down to its origin. Of course, you must do this before the stream separates from the wick and disperses in the air.

SCENE 14: HOW DO YOU LIKE YOUR EGGS—UP OR DOWN?

Action! Drop an egg into each of three tall clear cylinders or jars, filled with liquid. The egg sinks in the first jar, rises to the top of the liquid in the second, and settles in the middle of the third.

Someone may suggest that the eggs are different. Use a long-handled spoon or a fork to remove the eggs gently. Drop them into different jars. The results are the same. If anything is different, it must be in the jars, not in the eggs!

Props and Prep

   3 uncooked eggs
   3 tall clear cylinders or jars
   Salt (preferably coarse or Kosher salt for a clear solution)
   Large saucepan
   Long-stemmed funnel, thistle tube, or pipette (or a funnel
      with a piece of rubber or plastic tubing attached to the
      stem)

Prepare a saturated solution of salt water in the saucepan. This will require about 350 grams (12 ounces) of salt in 1 liter (about 1 quart) of water. The total amount of solution you prepare will depend on the size of the jars you use.

Fill the first jar with plain water.

Fill the second jar with the saturated salt solution.

Fill the third jar halfway with plain water. Then pour a layer of salt water *under* the water already in the third jar. To do this, put the long stem of a funnel (or a tube attached to the funnel), thistle tube, or pipette on the bottom of the jar. Let the saturated solution slowly run onto the bottom of the jar. This dense solution will form a layer of salt water below the plain water and remain there for days if undisturbed. If you try to pour the water onto the salt solution, there will be a considerable amount of mixing and you will not get a sharp boundary between the two layers.

Explanation

The density of an egg is more than that of water but less than that of saturated salt solution, so an egg sinks in plain water but floats in the salt solution.

SCENE 15: BLOWING THROUGH A BOTTLE

Action! Announce that you will blow out a candle by blowing *through* a bottle.

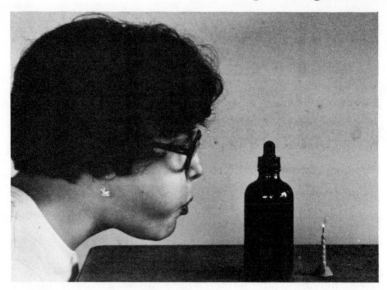

Light a candle and place it behind a wide bottle on a flat surface. Place your face in front of the bottle. Blow hard against the bottle. The candle will go out!

If your audience thinks you are cheating, let one of them do it. The results will be the same.

Props and Prep

Candle
Holder for candle
Wide bottle
Matches

Explanation

This scene illustrates Bernoulli's principle: where the speed of a fluid is great, the pressure within it is low; where the speed of a fluid is slow, the pressure within it is great.

The air you blow at the jar has a high speed so its pressure is low. As the air strikes the bottle, it divides into two streams. The higher pressure of the atmosphere holds the air streams against the sides of the bottle. The streams merge on the other side of the bottle, continue to move toward the candle, and push the flame (burning gases) from the wick.

SCENE 16: A COLLAPSING CAN

Action! Heat a large metal can on a burner, hot plate, or stove. Using a glove or a pot holder, remove the can when thoroughly hot and place on a heat-proof mat. Insert a cork in the can opening or replace its screw top. Cover the can completely with a cold, wet cloth. Strange creaking sounds emerge from beneath the cloth. Remove the cloth. The can has been crushed!

Props and Prep

Empty gallon metal can, with screw-top opening (the type used for solvents; see photo)
Cork or screw-on cap
Large piece of cloth or towel
Hot plate or stove
Pot holder or glove
Cold water
Heat-proof mat or newspaper

Rinse the can thoroughly before using to remove any flammable liquids that may still be in the can. Pour about a cup of water into the can and place it on the hot plate or stove about ten minutes before beginning this scene. Let the water boil for several minutes so that the steam can drive all the air from the can. Be sure to close the opening with a cork or cap the moment after you remove the can from the heat.

The heat-proof mat or thick newspaper will protect the table surface. **Always be very careful when using flames or hot plates.**

The cloth soaked in cold water speeds up the crushing process and adds to the mystery, but it is not essential. The can will be crushed, though more slowly, if simply left in the air.

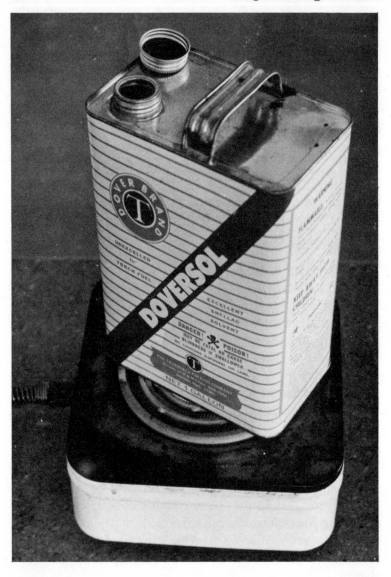

Explanation

As the closed, steam-filled can cools, the steam (water in the form of gas) condenses. This means there is less gas in the

can so the pressure inside decreases while the air pressure out-side the can remains the same.

Suppose the pressure inside the can drops to 4 pounds per square inch. The pressure outside is still about 14 pounds per square inch, and this means there is a net inward force of 10 pounds per square inch. If the can has an area of 230 square inches, the total inward force on the can will be 2,300 pounds —over a ton! No wonder the can is crushed!

SCENE 17: A COLORED GEYSER

Action! Put on a pair of gloves and announce that you are going to create a colored geyser. Remove a glass flask con-taining about 20 to 30 milliliters (1 ounce) of boiling water from a burner, stove, or hot plate. Close the flask with a sin-gle-hole stopper, with a long piece of glass or hard-plastic tub-ing running through it. One end of the tubing extends well into the flask. The other end is dipped into a beaker of colored water as you invert the flask, as shown in the picture.

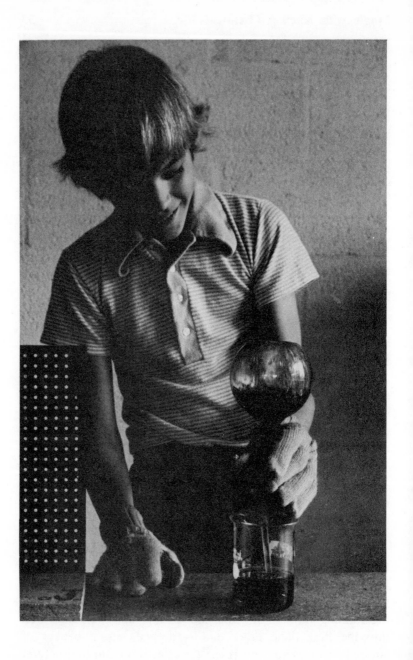

Very soon a spectacular "geyser" erupts as colored water rushes from the beaker, through the tube, into the flask.

Props and Prep

Pyrex glass flask (250 ml or larger, probably available from the science lab at school)
Single-hole stopper to fit flask
Glass or hard-plastic tubing (at least 20 cm [8 in.] long or 2 pieces joined by rubber tubing or tape)
Hot plate or other heat source
Food coloring
Gloves
Pyrex beaker or jar
Water
Glycerine or liquid soap

Lubricate the tubing with glycerine or liquid soap so it will slide through the hole in the stopper. **Be sure to wear gloves when you do this and hold the tubing close to the stopper** to avoid breaking it. **Be very careful! You can get bad cuts from broken tubing.** If the tubing is too wide, bore a larger hole through the stopper.

Let the water boil several minutes so steam can drive air out of the flask.

If you use a burner flame to heat the flask, be sure to keep it away from hair, clothing, and other flammable objects.

Do not heat any glass vessel unless it is made of Pyrex glass.

When you insert the stopper and invert the flask, get the tubing into the colored water as quickly as possible so that air does not re-enter the flask.

Explanation

When the steam from the boiling water in the flask cools, it condenses. With less gas inside, the pressure decreases. The air pressure outside the flask is then greater than the pressure within the flask, so water from the beaker is forced up the tube toward the low-pressure region. When the cool water reaches the flask, it causes the steam to condense even faster. This reduces the pressure in the flask very rapidly so water rushes in creating a "geyser."

SCENE 18: DON'T GET WET

Action! Lower a can or plastic bottle into a pail of water. When it is full, cover it with a plastic cap and take it out of the pail. No water flows from the can or bottle.

Ask someone to hold the can or bottle, for a moment. After he takes the container, he gets wet because water suddenly flows out a hole in the bottom of the can or bottle.

Props and Prep

> Plastic bottle (with cap) or metal can (with plastic cover that fits over its top)
> Nail
> Hammer
> Pail
> Water
> Vaseline

Punch a hole in the bottom of the can or bottle with a nail. Punch a second hole along the side of the can or bottle near the top.

If a can is used and the plastic cover does not seal tightly, spread a little Vaseline around the edge of the cover before you begin.

Explanation

When you remove the covered can (or bottle) from the pail, you hold your finger firmly over the hole near the top. A few drops will flow from the bottom of the can or bottle as you lift it. This reduces the pressure above the water in the can or bottle because the air there expanded when water left the can. The air pressure on the hole at the bottom of the can

is equal to the sum of the pressures from the column of water above the hole and the expanded air trapped above the water. Therefore, the water does not leave the can or bottle.

When you hand the container to the other person, remove your finger from the upper hole. Air enters this hole. The total pressure now of the air and water above the bottom hole becomes greater than air pressure outside, so water flows from the can or bottle.

SCENE 19: STRINGING WATER

Action! Tie one end of a wet string to the handle of a partly filled measuring cup or pitcher of water that has a narrow spout. Grasp the free end of the string, pull it over the spout, and hold taut over a jar or tumbler. Lift the pitcher and pour the water very slowly and carefully. The water runs along the

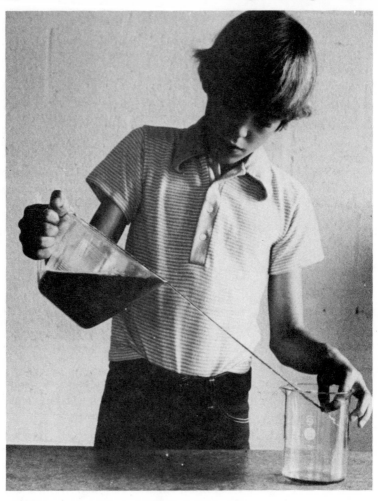

string into the jar. (Don't let go of the string, or the water will fall far short of the jar.)

You can repeat this scene using a long glass rod or a pencil in place of the string. Just place the glass rod or pencil across the top of an ordinary tumbler and pour. The water will flow along the rod or pencil.

Props and Prep

Measuring cup or pitcher with a narrow spout
Cotton string or long glass rod or pencil
Jar or tumbler
Water
Food coloring (optional; to make water more visible)

If you use string be sure it is *wet* before you pour the water.

Explanation

Water holds to the wet string, glass rod, or pencil because it is attracted to them and because water itself holds together very well. These forces of attraction between water and other materials and within water itself are strong enough to overcome the gravitational forces that tend to make the water fall.

Act V

Magic with Color, Light, and Shadows

For some scenes in this act you will need a light-box made of cardboard. You can make one quite easily. If you plan to do any scenes before a large audience, you may need two or three overhead or slide projectors to produce large shadows, images, or colored areas.

To make a light-box, take a cardboard box about 25 centimeters (10 inches) on a side. Remove the flaps where the box was opened. That will be the bottom of the box. Cut a small round hole on one side near the bottom of the box, big enough to hold a light socket for a clear 150-watt bulb with a straight filament, as shown in the picture. Such bulbs can be obtained from a hardware store. The photograph shows a view from the side of the box.

Cut rectangular openings at the bottom of the box about 8 by 10 centimeters (3¼ by 4 inches) in the other three sides —one in front of the bulb and one on each side of the bulb. Staple light cardboard or heavy paper strips around these openings to hold the various masks you will use to cover them.

Cut a few holes in the top of the box so heat can escape, as shown in the picture taken through the bottom of the box.

Make some masks for the light-box openings from black

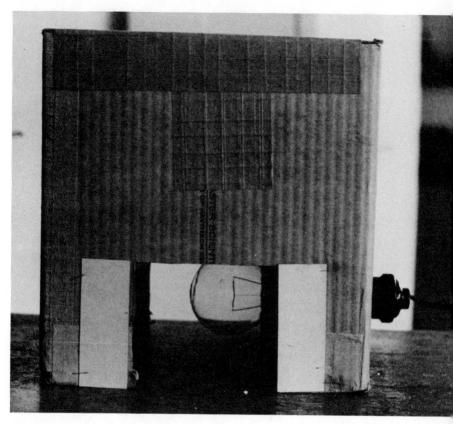

construction paper and others from transparent colored plastic, cellophane, or gelatin sheets. You will need sheets of the following colors for masks and colored light filters.

> Green
> Blue
> Red
> Yellow
> Magenta
> Cyan (blue-green)

For best results, I recommend the following colored sheets:

For green:	Roscolene No. 874 (medium green)
For blue:	Roscolene No. 863 (medium blue)
For red:	Roscolene No. 823 (medium red)
For yellow:	Roscolene No. 809 (straw)
For magenta:	Roscolene No. 837 (medium magenta)
For cyan:	Roscolene No. 858 (light green blue)

They may be obtained from Rosco Laboratories, Inc., 36 Bush Avenue, Port Chester, New York 10573. Colored sheets may also be obtained from Edmund Scientific Company, 617 Edscorp Building, Barrington, New Jersey 08007.

These colored sheets are expensive so you may prefer to buy less expensive smaller sheets from a local store.

The various masks you'll need should be about 10 by 12 centimeters (4 by 5 inches) to cover the openings in the box.

Unless you can get several overhead or slide projectors, the scenes in this act should be performed before a small audience. It would certainly be difficult for more than a dozen people to gather comfortably around a light-box and be able to see things clearly.

SCENE 1: PINHOLE GHOSTS (for a small audience)

Action! A light-box rests on a table, with its openings covered with black masks. (A hole has been punched in one of the black masks but the audience does not know it.) Darken the room. A glow from beneath the box indicates that there is some kind of light inside.

Say to the audience, "Let's see if we can get the bulb's spirit out of the box," and place a white screen several meters away from the black mask that has a hole in it. An image of the bulb's filament can be seen on the screen. As you move the screen nearer the box, the image grows smaller but brighter. As you move it away, the image grows larger and dimmer.

Ask the audience "Is there a single spirit or many? Let's see if they'll come out!"

Punch a new pinhole next to the one in the black paper mask. A second image suddenly appears on the screen! A third and still a fourth image appear as you punch two more holes close to the first one.

Now you say, "Let's see if we can put these spirits together!" Move a magnifying lens close to the pinholes. The images on the screen fuse to form a single "spirit"!

Props and Prep

  Light-box
  3 black masks (to cover the 3 openings in the light-box)
  Common pin or hatpin
  White screen (white paper taped to a sheet of cardboard)
  Magnifying lens (focal length 15 to 25 cm [6 to 10 in.];
      see Scene 7 for a method to determine the focal length of
      a lens)

Practice beforehand so you know about how far to place
the screen from the light-box in order to fuse the images with
the magnifying lens.

  One pinhole should be punched in one of the black masks
before the show begins. The room should be very dark.

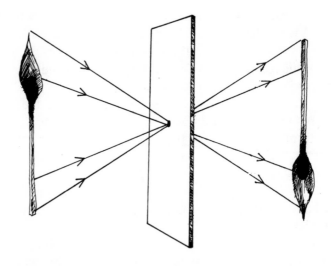

Explanation

  Because light travels in straight lines a bright object will
form an inverted image when its light rays travel through a
small hole onto a screen.

As you can guess from the drawing, the size of the image will depend on the distance of the screen and the object from the pinhole.

Two pinholes will form two images. The images can be fused with a magnifying lens because the lens, being convex, will bring all the light rays from the object together to form a real image (see Scene 7). This will work only if the lens is at least one focal length from the bulb in the box.

SCENE 2: MIXING COLORED LIGHT (for a small audience)

Action! In a very dark room, beams of red, blue, and green light emerge from the front side of a light-box. Place a white screen adjacent to that side at a slightly oblique angle. Using mirrors, reflect the beams onto the screen.

Where the red and green beams overlap on the screen, a yellow color appears. Where the red and blue beams overlap, a magenta color appears. Cyan appears where the blue and green beams overlap. A mixture of all three colored beams produces white light.

Props and Prep

Light-box
2 pocket mirrors
White screen (see Scene 1)
Mask with red, blue, and green transparent strips
2 black masks
Black construction paper

To make the mask shown in the diagram, cut three slots 2 centimeters (¾ inch) wide and 7 centimeters (2¾ inches) high in a piece of black construction paper made to fit the front opening in the light-box. Cover these slots with transparent green, blue, and red strips measuring 2½ by 9 centimeters (1×3½ inches). Tape the strips over the slots in the black paper. Then slide the entire mask between the strips

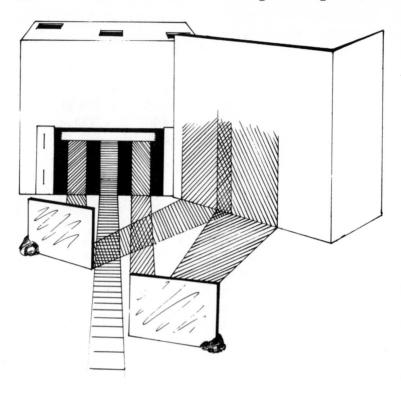

on each side of the opening. Cover the other two openings with black masks.

The intensity of the colored light on the screen can be changed by tilting the mirror or moving it closer to the light-box.

For a large audience, cover the stages of three overhead projectors with cardboard or black paper. Cut circular holes in the cardboard or paper and cover each with a colored sheet (one red, one blue, one green). By projecting the colored beams onto a screen, you can mix the colors as described for the light-box. Or you can use slide projectors and prepare red, green, and blue slides to make colored light beams.

This scene should be done at night or in a room that can be made very dark.

Explanation

Mixing colored lights in the manner described above is called "mixing by addition," because one color is added to another. The prime colors for light (not pigments) are red, green, and blue, because all other colors, including white, can be made by mixing these three.

The results of color addition are summarized in the color triangle below. See if they agree with your results.

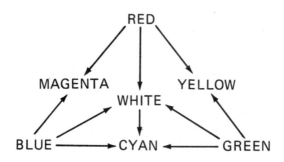

SCENE 3: COLOR IN COLORED LIGHT (for a small audience)

Action! Hold a square of green paper against a white screen and announce that you are going to change the green square to black. Turn the room lights out and the light-box on. The beam of red light comes from one side of the light-box. With a mirror, reflect part of the red beam onto the paper square on the screen. The screen is red but the green square is *black!*

Turn the room lights on and announce that you will turn a square of red paper black. Replace the red mask over the opening in the light-box with a green one and, turning off the room lights, repeat the actions above. The screen is green and the red square is *black!*

Repeating these procedures, change the colors of flags by reflecting first green and then red light onto a page of brightly colored flags held against the screen.

Props and Prep

White screen
Light-box
Red and green transparent masks
2 black masks
Red and green paper squares (soft, non-shiny)
Book with a page showing colored flags of different countries (in most encyclopedias)
Mirror

Before the scene begins, cover one opening in the light-box with a red transparent mask cut from a sheet of plastic, gelatin, or cellophane.

For a large audience you can use an overhead or slide projector to produce colored beams (see Scene 2).

Explanation

An object that is green in white light is green because it reflects only green light; it absorbs the other colors. If red light falls on a green object, the object absorbs the red light but does not reflect any light. Therefore, it appears black. Similarly, a red object reflects only red light. In green light it reflects no light and so appears black. Similarly, a blue object will appear black in red or green light.

Of course, things are seldom pure red, green, blue, or black, so there is usually a little reflected light from almost all objects, if you look closely. A smooth or shiny surface will also reflect some light regardless of its color.

SCENE 4: THE WORLD THROUGH COLORED FILTERS
(for a small audience)

Action! Invite your audience to look at different-colored objects and at the view through a window while holding colored masks in front of their eyes. Ask them to look at the page full of flags used in Scene 3 through the same masks.

Then ask them to look at the light coming through a window with cyan, magenta, and yellow masks, as well as red, green, and blue masks. Have them examine this same view through "sandwiches" made by placing the following masks on top of each other: cyan and yellow, cyan and magenta, yellow and magenta, all three (yellow, cyan, and magenta).

Props and Prep

Red, green, blue, cyan, magenta, and yellow transparent masks
Colored objects (pieces of non-shiny colored paper or a page of colored flags)
Window (preferably with view of the sky)

Cut the colored masks to such a size that each member of the audience can have a set of all six colors.

Explanation

The chart below lists the colors that will come through the different-colored masks, assuming the colors transmitted by the masks are pure.

Mask	*Color or colors transmitted in white light*
Blue	Blue
Green	Green
Red	Red
Cyan	Blue and green
Magenta	Blue and red
Yellow	Green and red

In this scene, colors are removed by substraction, that is, the masks absorb some colors and transmit the remaining ones. Putting two masks together is like an artist mixing pigments. The color that appears after the mixing is what remains after colors are substracted by masks or pigments. This is called the "substractive" method of color mixing.

A "sandwich" made of cyan and yellow masks allows only green light to pass. The cyan mask transmits only blue and green. The yellow mask transmits only green.

The chart below summarizes the results you can expect from all the mask (or filter) "sandwiches" suggested for the scene. They are what an artist would expect to find when he mixes the same pigments.

white light → |cyan filter| ⟶ blue + green light ⟶ |yellow filter| ⟶ green

white light → |magenta filter| ⟶ blue + red light ⟶ |yellow filter| ⟶ red

white light → |cyan filter| ⟶ blue + green light ⟶ |magenta filter| ⟶ blue

white light → |yellow filter| ⟶ red + green light ⟶ |cyan filter| ⟶ green light ⟶ |magenta filter| ⟶ black (no light)

A red mask will transmit only red light. Similarly, a green mask will transmit only green light, and a blue mask will transmit only blue light.

SCENE 5: LINGERING SHADOWS (for a small audience)

Action! Place a white screen near the light-box as shown in the drawing. With some clay, fasten a pencil in front of a green beam of light coming from the front opening in the light-box which you have covered with a green transparent mask. One of the side openings is covered with a red mask. The pencil's shadow cast on the screen is black. Move the pencil in front of the red beam and its shadow is still black. With the pencil in that position, take a mirror and reflect the green beam onto the pencil. The pencil will now cast two shadows, one red and the other green.

Move the pencil back to the green beam and reflect the red beam onto it. Again, you get two shadows, one red and the other green.

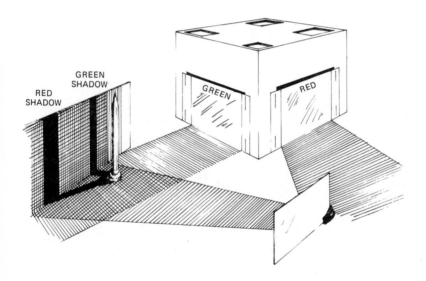

Now, tell your audience that if you remove the red mask and reflect white light on the pencil to obtain two shadows, the pencil will have a green shadow and the ghost of a red shadow, not a black one. When you do this, the audience sees a green shadow and a faint magenta shadow.

"Can you get a green shadow without the green light beam?" the audience may ask. Reply, "It's not a good day for green ghosts, but let's try!"

Use the red mask and reflected white light to produce two shadows. A red and a faint cyan shadow appear.

Props and Prep

> Light-box
> Red and green transparent masks
> Black mask
> Clay
> Mirror
> Pencil
> White screen

For a larger audience you can use overhead or slide projectors to produce larger colored beams. The projectors can be turned so that the beams overlap and give double shadows of an object held in the beams.

Explanation

A shadow on which red or green light shines will be red or green, respectively. But this does not explain why a shadow in white light is cyan if near a red shadow, nor why it is magenta in white light if near a green shadow.

It used to be thought that this effect was related to a tiring effect on the receptor cells in your retinas. But color photographs of these shadows show that they really *are* colored. (You might like to take some photographs to prove this to yourself.) A modern and rather complicated theory of color is needed to explain this phenomenon.

SCENE 6: INVERTED GHOSTS (for a small audience)

Action! Hold a round-bottomed flask near a light-colored wall or a white screen and invite your audience to look at the inverted "ghost" of the view seen through a window that appears on the wall or screen.

Repeat the scene using a magnifying lens. The "ghosts" of the outdoor view or, if at night, of a lamp appear inverted on the screen.

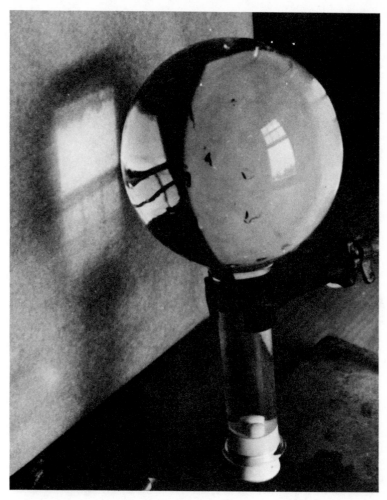

Props and Prep

    Round-bottomed flask (500 ml or 1 liter [1 pt or 1 qt])
    Screen or light-colored wall
    Magnifying lens
    Window with view or bright lamp in the room if at night

Explanation

The real image of a distant object will be found one focal length behind a convex lens. In fact, this is a good way to determine the focal length of a convex lens.

The light rays from objects far away are very nearly parallel when they strike a lens. A magnifying lens bends these rays inward. The rays are brought back together at a point very close to the focal length of the lens.

Notice how the two-dimensional convex lens shown in the picture brings together the nearly parallel rays from the right. (The two dark circles are screw heads used to hold the lens in place.) Can you explain the faint rays at the right side of the lens?

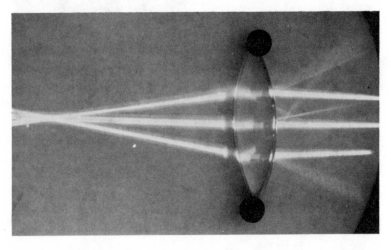

Because these images are formed by bringing back together light rays that came from each point on the object, they are called "real images." The light that forms the image is really there; it does not merely appear to be coming from the image as in the case of the "virtual images" that you see in ordinary flat mirrors. Virtual images cannot be focused on a screen, but real images as you have seen, *can* be focused on a screen.

SCENE 7: TURNING WORDS AROUND (for a small audience)

Action! Invite the audience to examine a number of large water-filled cylindrical pill bottles or test tubes that lie on their sides over white cards. Some bottles contain plain water, others contain green water. Under each bottle is a word. When the bottles filled with plain water are lifted a short distance above the words CAT, DOG, FAT, BOY, and GIRL, the words appear upside down. However, lifting bottles filled with green water seems to have no effect on the words they cover, which are BOX, OXIDE, and CHOICE.

Props and Prep

   8 large pill bottles or test tubes
   Caps for bottles or test tubes
   Hot water
   Food coloring
   White cards or paper strips with the words noted above printed on them

Completely fill the bottles or tubes with *hot* water. Add a drop of green food coloring to three bottles. Cap all the bottles. If there is a bubble in the bottle, it should be so small that it does not interfere with vision through the liquid. If cold water is used, bubbles will appear as the water warms because air is less soluble in warm water than in cold water.

Explanation

The cylindrical vessels bend light as shown in the picture of the lens in Scene 6 of this act.

While a magnifying lens is curved in all three dimensions so as to bring a beam of light to a point, the cylindrical lenses in this scene bring a beam of light together along a line rather than to a point.

Let your audience experiment with additional cylindrical lenses and hand lenses and move the bottles. After a while some of them may realize that BOX, OXIDE, and CHOICE consist of letters that are unchanged when inverted. The color of the lens has nothing to do with the results.

SCENE 8: A DISAPPEARING SHADOW (for a small audience)

Action! Hold a pencil so that it casts a sharp shadow on a screen or wall that is illuminated by an upright fluorescent light. When you turn the pencil 90 degrees, the shadow disappears.

Props and Prep

Pencil
Fluorescent light fixture with long bulb (a fluorescent desk lamp will do)
Screen or wall

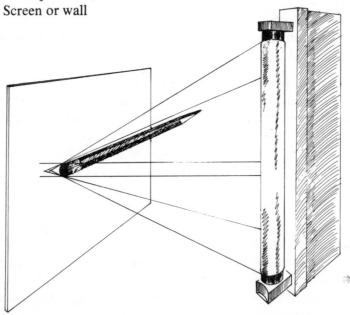

Explanation

The pencil will cast a shadow on the screen when it is held parallel with the axis of the fluorescent bulb. But if the pencil is perpendicular to the bulb's axis and parallel to the screen, its shadow is very dim because light from the ends of the bulb illuminate and cancel out the shadow, as shown.

SCENE 9: DISSOLVED LIGHT (for a small audience)

Action! Turn on a light or flashlight pointed right at the bottom of a large, covered glass jar lying on its side with its top near a sink. The jar is wrapped in dark paper and contains water.

Announce that you are going to make the light follow a stream of water. Then remove the piece of tape that covers the upper of two holes in the jar's lid, so that a stream of water flows into the sink through the bottom one. Hold a mirror in the sink so that the water stream hits it. When members of the audience look into the mirror, they will see that the light follows the water flowing out of the jar.

Props and Prep

    Large jar with screw-on cover
    Hammer
    Large nail
    Sink or large container
    Light bulb or bright flashlight
    Dark paper or wrapping paper
    Tape
    Mirror
    Water

Nearly fill the jar with water. Punch two holes in the jar's lid with a nail. The hole that will be near the bottom of the lid should be large—about ½ centimeter (¼ inch) in diameter —this is the opening for the water stream. The hole near the top of the lid can be smaller—it is simply a vent to admit air so water will flow from the jar.

Hold the mirror in the upper, *smooth* (unbroken) part of the stream because light disperses when the stream breaks up into drops. A large opening will ensure a reasonably long, smooth stream of water.

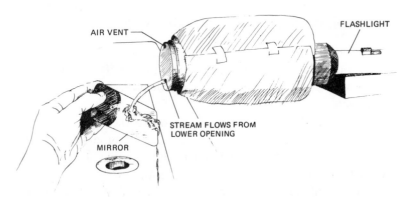

Explanation

You have made a light-pipe. Some of the light that enters the jar emerges in the flowing stream. This light is invisible to you; it is "trapped." When this light strikes the surface of the stream, it is reflected back into the stream. The only way you can see the light is to look up *into* the end of the stream. This you do by holding a mirror perpendicular to the flowing stream.

SCENE 10: AN UNDERWATER FLAME (for a small audience)

Action! Announce that you have succeeded in your search for a flame that burns underwater. Invite people to look through a small opening in a box where they can see a candle apparently burning in a beaker of water.

Props and Prep

Short candle (a few cm long)
Large cardboard box
Matches
Beaker or jar (taller than candle)
Piece of clear window glass
Water
Fire extinguisher or pail of water

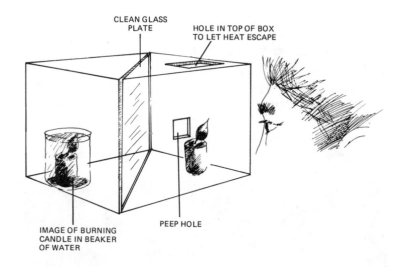

CLEAN GLASS PLATE

HOLE IN TOP OF BOX TO LET HEAT ESCAPE

IMAGE OF BURNING CANDLE IN BEAKER OF WATER

PEEP HOLE

The candle can be held in place with a few drops of hot wax. As for the box, cut away the flaps and place the open end over the candle, glass, and beaker as shown in the drawing. Cut a peephole near the center of one side of the box.

The drawing shows you how to arrange the materials so that the candle will appear to be in the beaker of water when someone looks through the peephole. (The artist has made the walls transparent so you can see what's inside.)

Before lighting the candle, be sure that it cannot be seen when you look through the peephole.

Be sure that the candle is away from the sides of the box and short enough so that the flame will not ignite the top of the box. Cut a hole in the top of the box above the candle to let the heat escape. Keep the box away from flammable objects. A fire extinguisher or a pail of water should be nearby in case the box accidentally catches fire.

Explanation

When you look in a flat mirror, your image, because of reflection, appears to be as far behind the mirror as you are in front of it. When you look through the peephole, you see the candle's image because some light from the candle is reflected by the glass back to your eye. The glass behaves like a mirror as does a window at night. The image of the candle is where the reflected light *appears* to be coming from—a position as far behind the glass as the candle is in front of the glass. If you place a beaker of water at the same location as the candle's image, the image will appear to be in the water.

As you can see in the picture, the reflected rays spread

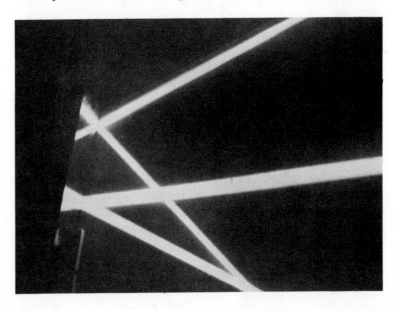

apart. They appear to come from a point behind the mirror. If you lay a couple of sticks or pencils along the reflected rays and extend them behind the mirror, you will find that they meet behind the mirror. Measure the distance from this point to the mirror. Then measure the distance from the mirror to the point of light from which the rays came. You will find that the distances are about the same.

A setup similar to the one in this scene but on a large scale is sometimes used to produce ghosts on a stage. A man dressed as a ghost stands just off stage. His image seems to appear on stage behind a large piece of glass at a 45-degree angle to the audience. The glass is so clean the audience cannot see it.

SCENE 11: THE MAGIC MIRROR (for a small audience)

Action! Invite members of the audience to look down into a box that holds a magic mirror that will make them stand on their heads.

When people look into the box, they see themselves upside down!

Props and Prep

2 mirrors (10 to 30 cm [4 to 12 in.] on a side)
Cardboard box, open at the top

Place the two mirrors in the box facing toward the opening so they form a V. The mirrors should be at right angles to one another. You can determine when the mirrors are at right angles by watching your own image as you adjust the mirrors. When the images near the line where the mirrors touch fuse to form a single upside-down image of your face, you will know they are at 90 degrees. Pieces of cardboard can be wedged between the box and the mirrors to hold the mirrors in place.

Explanation

Stand between two large mirrors that are at right angles to each other. You will see three images of yourself. The one in the middle is formed by double reflection. It is the image of an image. When you raise your right hand, the center image raises its right hand, too. It does not raise its left as normally happens when you look in a single mirror. This mirror arrangement puts your left side on the right side of the mirrors which is the left side of the image. Because such a mirror arrangement can turn a normal image right for left, it can also turn an image up for down when you look into the mirror with your mouth parallel to the line where the mirrors meet.

After people have seen themselves upside down, you might like to turn the cardboard box 90 degrees on its side and invite them to wink at their "normal" image. They will be surprised to see the image wink the same eye that they wink!

Act VI

The Magic of Galileo and Newton

Many of the major ideas of modern science were developed by Galileo and Newton in the seventeenth century. It was the work of these two men that unraveled the mysteries of motion. Once they had established a firm theory of motion and the forces that governed it, a great many natural phenomena including the motion of the moon, stars, and planets began to make sense.

The scenes in this act are based on the fundamental laws that were developed by Galileo and Newton or on laws related to or arising from their discoveries.

Most of the materials used in this act are things that you can find or make from articles around your own home.

SCENE 1: GALILEO AND THE PENDULUM: AN OPENER

Action! Mention to your audience that Galileo is regarded by some as the father of modern science and that one of his investigations began when he noticed that the time it takes a particular pendulum to swing over and back (its period) is the same for every swing. Demonstrate this with a pendulum 1 meter (39¼ inches) long. Let the pendulum with a lead bob at the end swing over and back five times. This will take 10 seconds. Now let the pendulum swing ten times. It now takes 20 seconds. The period of this pendulum is 2 seconds.

Now, mention that it looks as if the pendulum returns to the point from which it was released each time it comes back. Tell your audience you are so confident that it won't go higher that you will release the bob at the end of the pendulum from your nose, let the bob swing, and not flinch when it returns. The pendulum's return swing brings the bob close to your nose but does not touch it!

Ask your audience what they think will happen to the period of the pendulum if you replace the heavy bob with a light wooden one.

Replace the lead bob with a wooden bob and repeat the action. The periods of both are the same! Then ask, "What will happen to the period if we make the pendulum one half as long?" Most will think the period will either be halved or doubled. Shorten the pendulum from 1 meter to ½ meter (19⅝ inches). The period changes from 2 seconds to about 1.4 seconds. To make the period 1 second, change the length to ¼ of 1 meter, or 25 centimeters.

Props and Prep

> String
> Pendulum bobs (lead fishing sinker or heavy washer and a wooden bob about the same size)
> Clock or watch with a second hand
> Tape, C clamp, wooden slab, or hook (for hanging pendulum)
> Meter or yard stick

You will have to devise some way to suspend the pendulum. You might use tape on the top of a doorway, C clamps and a beam, a pair of wooden sticks to clamp the string, etc. Whatever method you use, be sure the support string does not *slide* at the point of suspension. The length of the pendulum, *l,* is measured from its point of support to the *center of the bob* as shown in the drawing.

You may want to have several pendulums if you can't change the pendulum's length easily.

A paper clip can be used to attach the bob to the string.

Explanation

The period of a pendulum is related to its length. The weight of the bob on that particular pendulum does not affect the period nor does the amplitude (size) of the swing over a fairly wide range.

To double the period of a pendulum, it must be four times as long. To triple the period, the pendulum must be nine times as long. As you can see, the period of the pendulum increases, not with its length but with the *square root* of its length!

SCENE 2: THE SWITCH AND THE TWIST

Action! Two washers or lead sinkers on strings hang below the bottom of a screen that hides the upper ends of these pendulums.

Pull one of the bobs slightly to one side and release it. It swings back and forth, but as it decreases its swing and finally stops the second bob takes on the motion. Then the motion returns to the first bob as the second slows down and stops. This exchange of motion continues for some time.

Say to the audience, "It seems that only one will dance at a time. Let's see if that can be changed." You reach behind the screen and make an adjustment before releasing one bob again. This time the "dancers" dance together, but they switch from a to-and-fro motion to "the twist." Again the motion keeps changing. This time from a back-and-forth to a twisting action.

Props and Prep

    Long pencil or stick
    String
    Steel washers or lead fishing sinkers
    Tape
    Chair
    Cardboard or paper screen

The photograph shows how you should set up the double pendulum behind the screen.

To make the "dancers" do "the twist" you move the stick down closer to the bobs.

The screen can be taped to a heavy board that rests on the seat of the chair and extends a short way beyond the front end.

Explanation

As you can see in the picture, a stick connects one pendulum with the other. Each string is wrapped once around the stick. The energy of motion is transferred from one pendulum to the other through the stick. Why the motion switches from back and forth to the twist when the stick is close to the bob is very difficult to explain.

SCENE 3: AN UNDECIDED PENDULUM

Action! Hang a bob on a long spiral spring, pull it down, then release it. As the bob moves up and down explain that this is another kind of pendulum—a spring pendulum. Its period is also constant for different amplitudes. But, unlike a swinging pendulum, its period *does* depend on the weight of the bob.

Hang heavier and lighter weights on the spring to show that the period is related to the weight of the bob. As the weight increases, the period becomes longer.

Finally, mention that there are some weights and springs that don't "know" whether they are spring pendulums or ordinary pendulums. Pull a weight from your pocket, hang it on the spring, and start it moving. The spring bobs up and down; then it begins to swing as it bobs; then it swings without bobbing; then it swings and bobs again and returns to its original motion. These changes of motion are repeated over and over. The picture shows a spring that is in its swinging phase. The top of the spring is attached to a special clamp that extends from the long vertical rod.

Props and Prep

    Spiral spring (about 30 to 50 cm [12 to 20 in.] long)
    Pendulum bobs (various weights)
    Nail, hook, C clamp, etc. (for hanging pendulum)

You will have to experiment to find the right weight bob that makes the spring swing as well as bounce. When you get just the right weight, there will be a short time where all bouncing will cease and the spring just swings like an ordinary pendulum. You may have to tape several smaller bobs together to get just the right weight. Have the right weight bob in your pocket at the start of the scene.

Explanation

The period of a particular spring pendulum increases with the square root of the weight you hang on it. To make the period twice as long you must make the weight four times as large.

For any particular spring pendulum, there is a particular weight bob that makes the pendulum swing as well as bounce. This bob will stretch the spring pendulum to such a length that its period is exactly the same as the period of an ordinary pendulum of identical length. With this particular bob, the pendulum can't "decide" whether to swing back and forth or bounce up and down. The period of both motions are the same.

SCENE 4: FALLING TOGETHER

Action! Hold a heavy object such as a baseball in one hand and a light object such as a tennis ball or marble in the other. Extend your arms and release both balls at the same time. They will hit the floor together.

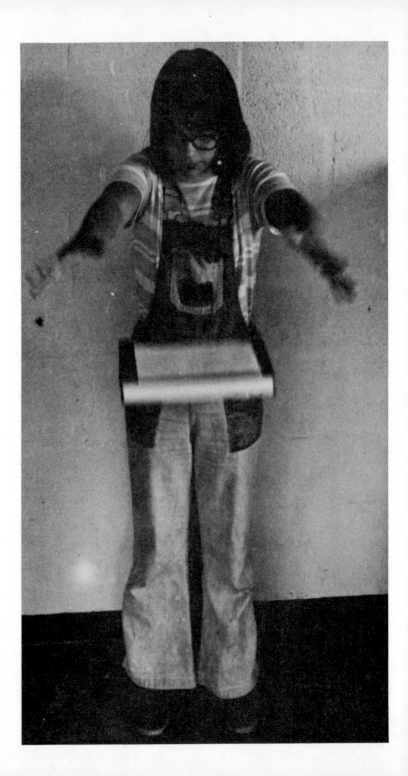

Then tell your audience the story of Galileo and the Leaning Tower of Pisa and how he found that two objects will fall at the same rate even if their weights are quite different.

Then take a book in one hand and a piece of paper in the other, and release them both at the same time. The book falls to the floor much faster than the paper. You then place the paper on top of the book and drop them. The paper and the book fall together as you can see in the photograph.

Props and Prep

Heavy object (baseball, hammer, stone, etc.)
Light object (tennis ball, marble, nail, etc.)
Book
Piece of paper (slightly smaller than the book)

Explanation

Galileo's discovery that all objects, regardless of their weight, fall at the same rate is true only in a vacuum or when air resistance is negligible.

A piece of paper has a large area for its weight so its rate of falling is greatly reduced by the air resistance. If the paper is placed on top of the book, the book shields the paper from the air.

Any object falling through the air will stop speeding up (accelerating) and reach a steady speed called its "terminal velocity" after a while. A sky diver reaches a terminal velocity of about 190 kilometers (120 miles) per hour after falling for about 12 seconds. The upward push of the air on the sky diver increases as his or her speed increases. When the upward force due to the air resistance becomes equal to the sky diver's weight, he or she falls with a steady speed.

SCENE 5: CATCH A FALLING BUCK

Action! Tell the audience that if anyone of them thinks he can catch a dollar before it falls through his fingers, he can

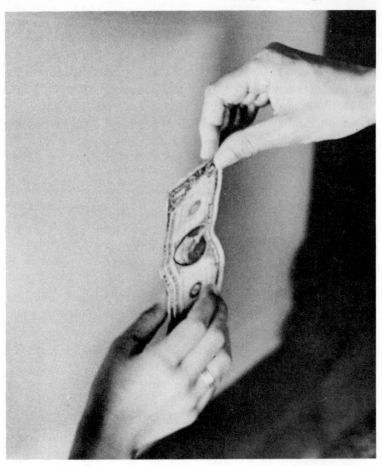

keep the bill. You show them what you mean by holding a
dollar bill with the index finger and thumb of one hand. You
place the same fingers of your other hand about 5 centimeters
(2 inches) above the bottom of the bill and release it with
your right hand. You easily catch the bill with your left hand.

Tell the volunteer to hold his fingers where those on your
second hand were and to watch your other thumb and finger.
When he sees you release your grip, he should try to catch the

dollar as it falls between his fingers. He is not allowed to move his hand downward or to anticipate your release. If he does neither, he will never catch the bill.

Props and Prep

Dollar bill (preferably new)

Explanation

A dollar bill is about 15 centimeters (6 inches) long. As the person trying to catch the bill holds his finger about 5 centimeters (2 inches) above the bottom of the bill, he must react before the bill falls 10 centimeters (4 inches). It only takes 0.15 second for the bill to fall this far. Few, if any, people can react this fast.

It's easy for you to catch the bill yourself because your one hand knows when your other hand will release the bill. You don't have to watch someone else's fingers and react to them. Your brain can send a signal to the second hand at the same moment it sends one to your first hand.

SCENE 6: FLIGHT TIME OF A BULLET

Action! Tell your audience that one of Galileo's discoveries was that an object fired in a horizontal direction will fall the same distance in one second as an object that is simply dropped straight downward.

To demonstrate this, place two coins or washers near the edge of a table. Part of one coin or washer should extend beyond the edge. Ask the audience to listen to see if they can tell which coin lands first when you slide the second coin or washer into the first one at a slight angle. (If the second one hits straight on, it will stop and not leave the table.) Both objects leave the table, but one falls nearly straight downward while the other travels some distance from the table. They will find that both coins hit the floor at the same time.

Of course, many will not be convinced because the coin isn't really a bullet—so you go on!

You hold a loaded dart gun and ask someone to place a second dart on the one in the gun as shown in the photograph.

Have your assistant check to be sure the gun is level. He can align the gun barrel with something horizontal, such as a window frame, behind the gun.

Ask the audience to watch and listen to see if they can tell which "bullet" lands first. Fire the gun. Both "bullets" hit the floor at the same time!

Props and Prep

> Table
> 2 coins or washers
> Gun for suction-cup darts
> 2 darts

Explanation

The vertical motion of an object due to gravity is independent of its horizontal motion. If the gun is fired *horizon-*

tally over a *level* surface, it will take the same time for both "bullets" to strike the floor despite the fact that one, because of its horizontal motion, travels a lot farther than the other one.

How will the flight times compare if the "bullet" is fired at an upward angle? At a downward angle? These questions might be added to the scene. Experiments to answer these questions would enable the audience to see that they really can distinguish between flight times when the loaded "bullet" is *not* fired horizontally.

SCENE 7: COINS FROM UNDER (for a small audience)

Action! Place a stack of six to eight nickels or quarters near the edge of a smooth table. Announce that you will remove the bottom coin without touching the others.

You slide the blade of a table knife swiftly along the surface of the table "through" the bottom coin. The bottom coin is knocked out from under the others as shown in the photograph.

You can repeat this process until only one coin remains.

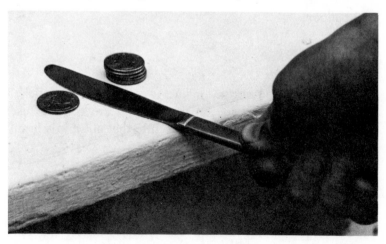

Props and Prep

Table
6 to 8 nickels or quarters
Table knife

Explanation

This scene illustrates the principle of inertia. The force you exert with the knife acts only on the bottom coin. Since there is no force on the other coins, they remain in position. Of course, if there were a lot of friction between the coins, the whole pile would move.

SCENE 8: A BALLOON THAT WON'T EXPLODE

Action! Hand someone an inflated balloon and a pin and ask him or her to prick the balloon and make it burst.

After the bang, pick up another inflated balloon yourself and carefully insert a pin into it. The balloon does not break!

Props and Prep

2 balloons
2 pins
Clear plastic tape
Tie bands

Before the scene begins, inflate two balloons and stick a piece of clear plastic tape on the one *you* are going to use. Rub the tape with your finger to be sure that all of it is firmly stuck to the balloon's surface.

Explanation

When you stick the pin into your balloon, you push it through the *center* of the clear tape. The tape prevents the balloon from ripping around the pinhole; hence, the only place air can escape is through the tiny pinhole.

SCENE 9: A DANCING BALL

Action! Adjust the hose of a vacuum cleaner so that it is blowing rather than sucking air. Ask someone to hold the hose so that the air is blown upward in a vertical stream.

Gently place a Ping-pong ball in the air stream. The ball remains suspended there, "dancing on air."

Then place the same ball in a glass funnel *while you blow downward through the funnel's stem,* as shown in the photograph. The ball twists and turns but remains in the open funnel even though you are blowing *downward.* When you stop blowing, the ball falls to the floor.

Props and Prep

Vacuum cleaner
Ping-pong ball
Glass funnel

Explanation

Both parts of this scene illustrate Bernoulli's principle—when the velocity of a fluid is high, the pressure is low; when the velocity of a fluid is low, the pressure is high.

Air flowing around the ball in either part of the scene is moving quite fast. Therefore, the pressure near the ball is less than the air pressure outside the stream. Whenever the ball begins to move out of the stream it encounters a high pressure area that pushes it back into the low pressure zone.

Of course, you could not use a heavy ball for this scene. Do you know why?

SCENE 10: UP AND DOWN SUBMARINE

Action! Place your hand on a corked bottle that contains a floating medicine dropper and say, "Down submarine!"

The medicine dropper sinks to the bottom of the bottle. Then say, "Up submarine!" The medicine dropper rises to the surface.

Finally, say, "Half-way submarine!" The medicine dropper stays suspended between the bottom and the top of the bottle.

Props and Prep

Tall, clear glass jar or bottle
Stopper to fit jar or bottle
Eyedropper
Water

Fill the jar almost to the top with water. Fill the eyedropper with just enough water so that it floats in the jar with just the tip of the rubber bulb above the water.

Place the stopper in the mouth of the jar, but do not push it down into the neck.

Explanation

When you push down on the cork, you compress the small volume of air in the jar. This increase in pressure is "felt" by the water too, and forces more water up into the eyedropper, so that it sinks. By removing your hand or reducing your push

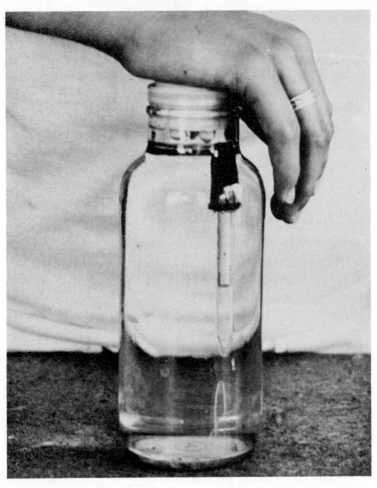

on the stopper, the pressure within the jar will force the stopper up. An object in a liquid is buoyed up by a force equal to the weight of the liquid it displaces. (This is called "Archimedes' principle.") The buoyant force on the eyedropper is enough to make it float. When the added water enters, it makes the weight of the dropper greater than the buoyant force, so the dropper sinks.

With practice, you can learn to push the stopper just enough to control the pressure so that the dropper will remain suspended in the middle of the jar.

SCENE 11: A BED OF NAILS

Action! Tell the audience that you have recently returned from India where you learned to control your reaction to pain.

To demonstrate this miraculous power, remove your shoes and stand in your stocking feet, or better yet your bare feet, on a bed of nails.

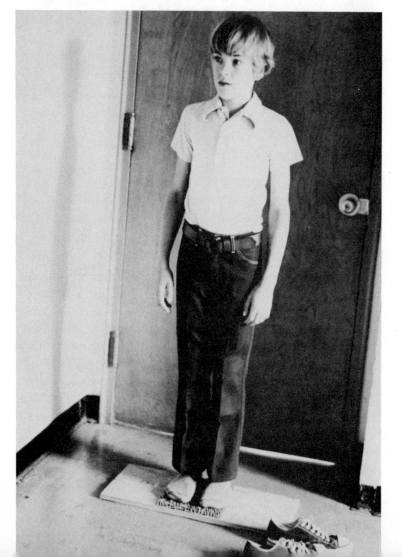

Props and Prep

> 1,600 nails (2½ to 3 cm [1 to 1¼ in.] long)
> Plywood board (1½ to 2 cm [½ to ¾ in.] thick and 30
> cm [1 ft] or more square)
> Electric drill
> Hammer

Draw a grid 25 centimeters (10 inches) square in the center of the board, with lines 6 millimeters (¼ inch) apart running perpendicular to each other. This will leave a border around the grid. Drill (or have an adult drill) holes through the board at the intersections of these lines. The holes should be a little smaller than the diameter of the nails you will drive through the holes. That means you will have to drill about 1,600 holes and drive 1,600 nails—a lot of work! The scene is very effective, but it takes a lot of stamina to prepare for it the first time you do it. However, if you build the bed a little bit each day, it's not so bad, especially when you realize that once made, the bed will last for years.

Explanation

If you tried to stand on a few nails far apart, the pressure on your feet at the tip of each nail would be so great that the nails would penetrate your flesh. With a large number of nails, your weight is distributed over many more nails so the force on each nail is not nearly enough to penetrate your flesh.

Push a pencil point against your hand; you can feel it hurt. But if you turn the pencil around and push the blunt end against your hand just as hard, you barely feel it, because the force of the pencil is spread out over a much bigger area.

SCENE 12: A MYSTERIOUS PAIR OF BALLOONS

Action! Hold up two balloons before your audience. The necks of both balloons are attached to a rubber stopper or a wooden spool. One balloon has been blown up a lot, the other has been blown up just a little. A band has been tied around the neck of the smaller balloon to prevent air from moving between them.

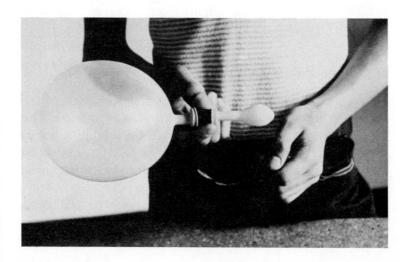

You ask, "What will happen when I remove the tie band?"

Most people will say that air will move from the big balloon to the small one.

When you remove the band, air moves *from the small balloon to the large one!*

The small balloon at the right side of the picture was about twice as big before the tie band was removed.

Props and Prep
   2 round balloons (same size)
   Wooden spool
   Tie band
   Rubber stopper or empty wooden thread spool

Blow up one balloon a little. Tie it off by wrapping a tie band around its neck; attach the neck to one end of a stopper or spool. Blow up the second balloon to a large size and attach its neck to the other end of the spool or stopper.

Explanation

The pressure in a small balloon is greater than the pressure in a balloon that has been stretched to a large size. This. is why it's so hard to blow air into a balloon when you first start to fill it. After you've made it quite large, it's easier to blow air into it.

SCENE 13: CARD AND CLOTH

Action! Announce to your audience that both parts of this scene are illustrations of Newton's first law of motion. This law states that a moving body will remain in motion at a constant velocity unless acted on by an outside force. Explain that you are going to deal with two special cases of that law in which the velocity of a body is zero.

Lay a small card on the mouth of an empty soda bottle. Then carefully place a large marble on the card so that it is right over the opening of the bottle.

Give the card a sharp snap with your fingers. The card flies out but the marble remains in place, resting on the mouth of the bottle.

Now move to a card table covered with a plastic cloth. On one side of the table are plastic plates and plastic cups or tumblers filled with water.

Grab the end of the table cover on the side opposite the dishes and give it a quick horizontal pull. The cloth comes off the table but the dishes remain in place!

Props and Prep

Soda bottle
Small card
Large marble
Card table with smooth surface
Plastic table cloth (or newspaper)
Plastic dishes

You'll have to practice this scene a number of times. Both parts are effective if done correctly.

You may want to place the card on the bottle so that the end you snap is closer to the bottle than the other end, as shown in the photograph.

When you pull the table cover from under the dishes, you must pull it *straight out,* parallel to the table, and *very quickly.* Don't pull *downward*—you'll send dishes flying.

Explanation

Since any object at rest tends to stay at rest unless acted on by an outside force and since the friction between the marble and the card and between dishes and the tablecloth is marginal, the forces you exert on the card and the tablecloth will not be transmitted to the objects resting on them.

SCENE 14: A FRICTIONLESS AIR CAR

Action! As in Scene 13, tell the audience that Newton's first law of motion states that a moving body will remain in motion at constant velocity unless acted on by an outside force. Tell them that we seldom see this law in action because friction (an outside force) usually causes moving things to slow down.

Then say, "But today, you *will* see a body move at constant speed."

Blow up a balloon and attach it to a wooden spool glued to a square piece of wood. Give this "air car" a little push. It glides along a smooth level surface at a constant, slow speed, until you stop it and push it back.

Props and Prep

Round balloon
Empty wooden spool
Glue
Tie band

Piece of plywood (6 mm [¼ in.] thick and 6 to 7 cm [2½ in.] square)
Sandpaper
Drill
Long, level, smooth surface (formica or glass table top)

Sand the bottom of the plywood square until it is very smooth on one side. Sand the edges so they are slightly rounded.

Drill a 1½-millimeter (¹⁄₁₆-inch) hole in the very center of the square. Glue the spool to the unsanded top of the square. Be sure the hole in the spool is in line with the hole in the wooden square.

You may want to have someone help you when you place the balloon on the spool. A tie band wrapped around the neck of the balloon will help keep the air in it while you attach it to the spool.

Explanation

Air emerging from the hole in the bottom of the square forms an air cushion between the plywood square and the surface of the table. Thus it slides, reducing friction to almost zero. After you give the air car a push, there is practically no force slowing it down so it continues to move along at a constant speed. Of course, if the surface is not level, you will see the car speed up, slow down, or move to one side as the force of gravity changes its motion.

SCENE 15: STRENGTH ISN'T EVERYTHING

Action! Bet someone in the audience who looks much stronger than you that with one finger you can prevent him from placing the end of a broom handle on a small target on the floor. Explain that you will hold your finger on the end of the handle, while he will hold both hands as close to the straw part of the broom as possible.

When he tries to put the end of the handle on the target as you push your finger against the handle, he finds the task impossible!

Props and Prep

Broom
Small target (tape, lid, or card)

Explanation

The broom handle acts as a lever. The fulcrum is one of the strong person's hands. His other hand supplies the force, F, but that force is very near the fulcrum. The force that you exert, f, is far from the fulcrum.

The product of his force, F, and the distance of that force from the fulcrum, d, called the "moment of force" about the fulcrum. His moment of force, $F \times d$, can be balanced by an equal moment of force in the opposite direction. So if you exert force f at distance D from the fulcrum, your moment of force about the fulcrum is $f \times D$. If $f \times D = F \times d$, the handle will not move.

Suppose he exerts a force of 50 kilograms (110 pounds)

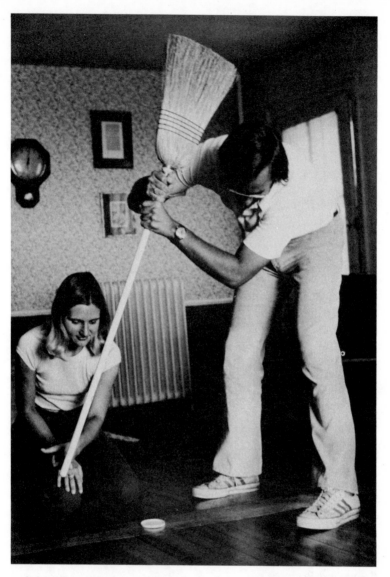

weight 10 centimeters (4 inches) from the fulcrum. You can balance that moment of force if you exert only 5 kilograms (11 pounds) weight at a distance of 100 centimeters (40 inches) from the fulcrum.

$$50 \times 10 = 5 \times 100$$

SCENE 16: UP AND OVER

Action! Show the audience that the small pail you hold contains some water. Then announce that you can turn the pail upside down and the water will not fall out.

Grasping the pail's handle, you swing it slowly in a vertical circle. At the top of the circle the pail is upside down but the water stays in the pail.

Props and Prep

Pail
Water

Explanation

When you swing the pail, you provide an inward force on it —a centripetal force. If you swing the pail at a rate greater than about once every 2 seconds, the centripetal acceleration at the bottom of the pail throughout its motion is greater than the downward acceleration of the water due to gravity. Since your force accelerates the pail more than gravity accelerates the water, the water cannot leave the pail.

SCENE 17: A CENTER-SEEKING FLAME

Action! Light a small birthday candle at the end of a wooden arm that extends from a turntable. Place a plastic chimney or cylinder over the candle and set the turntable in motion. The rotating flame is deflected inward as shown in the photograph.

Props and Prep

Small birthday candle
Turntable for record player
Stick of wood (about 1 cm by 5 cm by 140 cm [½ in. by 2 in. by 4½ ft])

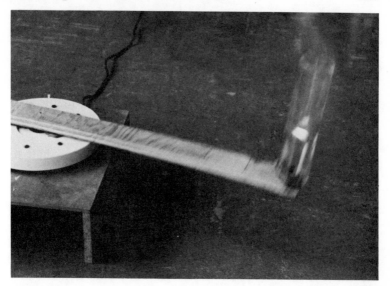

Clay
Clear glass or plastic chimney or cylinder (about 15 cm [6 in.] high and 5 to 8 cm [2 to 3¼ in.] in diameter)
C clamp or weight (to balance candle and chimney on other end of board so that board will not tip to side of candle)
Matches
Drill

Drill a hole in the center of the stick so it will fit over the spindle in the center of the turntable. Fasten the candle to one end of the board with a piece of clay. Cover the candle with the clear cylinder; fasten in place with clay or tape. Let the chimney extend a little bit over the end of the stick so air can enter the bottom of the chimney. An identical setup can be built at the other end of the board, or you can attach a weight there to balance the board so it doesn't tip toward side of the candle and chimney.

When you are ready to begin, remove the chimney, light the candle, replace the chimney, and start the turntable. Set to medium speed.

The long wooden arm enables the audience to see the flame pointing inward very clearly. The same effect can be obtained by having a shorter arm and a faster rotating turntable, but then the audience cannot see the effect as clearly because the candle moves too fast.

If you are mechanically inclined, you can build a shaft to support the board and simply spin it by hand.

Be very careful with matches and flame involved in this scene.

Explanation

There is an inward, or centripetal, force exerted on the candle when it rotates on the turntable. The flame is less dense than the air around it and so moves inward. (See the next scene for a more detailed explanation.)

SCENE 18: ROUND AND ROUND

Action! Explain to the audience that they will be able to understand the two previous scenes better if they watch this one carefully.

Show them a giant accelerometer like the one in the picture. Tell the audience that the cork in the accelerometer always moves in the direction of the acceleration (an increase in speed) or the deceleration (a decrease in speed). Show this to be true by moving the accelerometer along a horizontal path perpendicular to the audience's line of vision. When you speed up the jar, the cork moves forward. When you slow it down, the cork moves backward in a direction opposite to that of the motion and in the direction that the speed is *decreasing*.

When you hold the jar and move it in a circle, the cork moves toward the center of the circle, showing that the acceleration is inward.

Props and Prep

    Gallon jar
    Cap. for jar
    Cork
    String
    Tape
    Common pin
    Water

Tie a string to the pin and put the pin into the cork so that the head of the pin holds the string to the cork. Tape the other end of the string to the center of the jar cap. (A smaller accelerometer is shown in the second picture.)

Be sure that the string plus the cork is shorter than the jar is deep.

Fill the jar with water. Place the cork and string on the water's surface and carefully screw on the cap. Invert the jar, and presto!!—the accelerometer is made!

Explanation

The water in the jar has more inertia than the cork. When you move the jar forward, the water tends to stay where it is. Thus, there is an increase in pressure on the liquid at the back of the jar and a decrease in the front. The cork responds to this pressure difference and moves forward. The reverse holds true when the speed of the jar decreases. The water tends to keep moving, increasing the pressure at the front of the jar, while the cork moves backward.

SCENE 19: COMPASS MAGIC (for a small audience)

Action! Place a magnetic compass on a wooden table or on the floor. (Keep it away from steel or iron objects.) The compass needle will point in a northerly direction.

Move a magnet in the vicinity of the compass, and the needle responds by moving either clockwise or counterclockwise. Move wood, plastic, copper, or aluminum objects around the compass. They will have no effect on the needle. By bringing your right hand near the compass, show that flesh is not magnetic.

Next, hold a long steel rod near the compass. The rod has little effect on the needle. Hold the rod parallel to the compass needle with the end of the rod which points north tipped downward so that the rod is parallel to the earth's magnetic field. Strike the rod sharply with a hammer. When you again bring the rod close to the compass, it is clear that the rod has become magnetic because the needle will move. In fact, you can make the needle turn in circles by moving the end of the rod around the compass.

To eliminate the rod's magnetism, turn it so that it is aligned along an east–west axis and drop it on the floor several times. After this, the rod again has little effect on the compass needle when it is brought close to the compass.

Now, lay a piece of copper wire on top of the compass so the wire is parallel to the compass needle. The wire is clearly not magnetic because it has no effect on the compass needle. Tape the ends of the wire to hold it in place. When you connect the ends of the wire to the poles of a battery for a moment, the compass needle suddenly turns so it is nearly perpendicular to the wire. Somehow the wire has been magnetized!

After removing the wire, bring your left hand near the compass and the needle goes wild. Say, "I guess I've become magnetized by working with all these magnetic objects. Let's see if it's catching."

Touch someone and have him bring his hand near the compass. There is very little effect.

Props and Prep

   Magnetic compass
   Steel rod (1 to 2 m [3 to 6 ft] long
   Hammer
   Bar magnet
   Small rubberized magnet
   Wood, plastic, copper, and aluminum objects
   Copper wire (about 15 cm [6 in.] long)
   Flashlight battery
   Adhesive tape

Tape the small magnet to the underside of your wrist-watch band.

Explanation

Wood, plastic, copper, and aluminum are not magnetic and cannot be made magnetic.

When a steel (or iron) rod is held parallel to the earth's magnetic field and struck with a hammer, the atoms in the rod (which are, in effect, tiny magnets themselves) line up along the lines of the earth's magnetic field. The rod is now magnetic. The effect is similar to tapping a compass needle that's stuck. When freed, the needle lines up in a north–south direction along the earth's magnetic field. Each of the atoms in the iron rod may be thought of as a tiny compass needle or magnet. When jarred, some of them will line up like a long line of bar magnets.

Dropping the rod when it is aligned along an east–west axis jars the magnetic arrangement of the atoms. Of course, they might line up across the axis of the rod, but then the north and south poles of all these short magnets would be side by side. Their like poles would repel, causing them to turn away from each other.

When the wire carries an electric current, there is a magnetic field around the wire. This is true for any electric current and is the principle on which electric meters and electric motors are built.

You, of course, cannot become magnetic by handling magnetic objects, but you can hide a small rubberized magnet under a watch band or bracelet on your left wrist. Extend this bit of trickery by showing your audience that while your left hand is magnetic, your right hand is not. If they don't suspect something after that, they deserve to be fooled!

SCENE 20: AN UNDERWATER LIGHT

Action! Hold up a lighted flashlight bulb that is connected to two, three, or four D Cells in series and ask the audience, "What do you think will happen if I place this bulb and its holder in this beaker of water?" Most people think the bulb will go out under water.

When you lower the bulb into a beaker of water, it continues to glow. Then ask, "What will happen if I add some salt to the water?" Again, most people think it will surely "short out" in salt water. Add the salt, but it has no effect on the bulb,

other than some bubbling around the connections to the bulb
holder.

Props and Prep

   Flashlight bulb
   Bulb holder

D cell or small 6-volt battery made from a pack of 4 D cells
(see photograph)
2 clip-leads
Rubber bands (to hold D cells together to make a battery)
Glass or tumbler
Water
Salt (preferably kosher salt)

WARNING!!! Do not try this experiment with ordinary lamp bulbs plugged into a wall socket. Use nothing larger than a 6-volt battery of D cells.

Explanation

Most people think a bulb will go out in water and certainly in salt water. However, the wires in, and leading to, the bulb are much better conductors of electricity than water or salt water, so very little electricity flows through the water.

SCENE 21: AN ORNERY BULB (for a small audience)

Action! Connect two pink-beaded minature radio bulbs in series with two D cells as shown in the drawing. Both bulbs light. Replace the bulbs with white-beaded radio bulbs. Both of these bulbs light too. Now, place one bulb of *each* lot in the socket. Only one of the bulbs lights, as shown in the photograph.

Suggest that the bulb with the white bead in it is "ornery" and will light only when paired with one like itself.

Ask the audience for their suggestions. Try whatever they suggest. Only the bulb with the pink bead will light when in series with the bulb with the white bead.

What happens if the two bulbs are wired in parallel—that is, side by side as shown in the drawing?

Props and Prep

  2 GE ✕48 bulbs (pink beads)
  2 GE ✕41 bulbs (white beads)
  3 clip-leads
  2 bulb holders
  2 D cells
  Battery case or rubber band (to hold D cells together and
    clip-leads to poles of D cells)

D CELLS

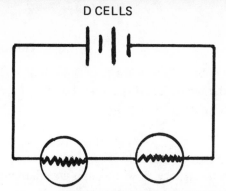

BULBS IN SERIES

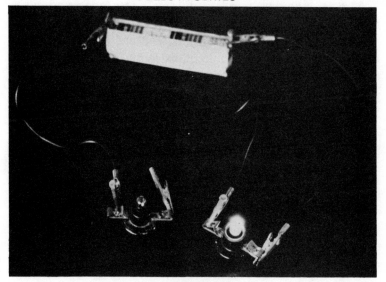

D CELLS

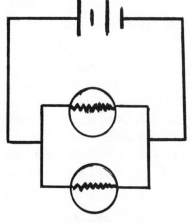

BULBS IN PARALLEL

The first two bulbs used are GE ☀48 bulbs. The second two used in the scene are GE ☀41 bulbs. These are radio bulbs, *not* flashlight bulbs.

Explanation

A ☀48 bulb has a relatively large resistance. This means it lets very little electricity flow through its filament each second, but that is enough to light this bulb.

A ☀41 bulb has a relatively small resistance and takes more electricity to make it glow.

When the two different bulbs, a ☀48 and a ☀41, are connected in series, the ☀48 bulb offers so much resistance to the flow of electricity that there is not enough current (number of electrical charges flowing by a point per second) to make the ☀41 bulb glow.

SCENE 22: BENDING WATER

Action! Ask your audience, "Have you ever seen water bend? Watch this!"

Rub a "magic wand" with some woolen cloth. When the wand is held near a small stream of water flowing from a tap, the stream is bent dramatically! The water seems to be attracted to the magic wand as shown in the photograph.

Props and Prep

Water tap
Rubber rod, plastic ruler, or plastic comb
Woolen cloth

This scene will work best when there is low humidity. It's not a scene to try in midsummer. If the air is very dry, you may be able to bend the water with your finger. In that case, stand on large glass jars that serve as insulators. Have someone rub your hand with some woolen cloth. Then bring your finger near the stream and watch the water bend toward you.

The "magic wand" mentioned in the *Action* can be a hard-rubber rod, a plastic ruler, or a plastic comb. The wand can be charged by rubbing it with a woolen cloth.

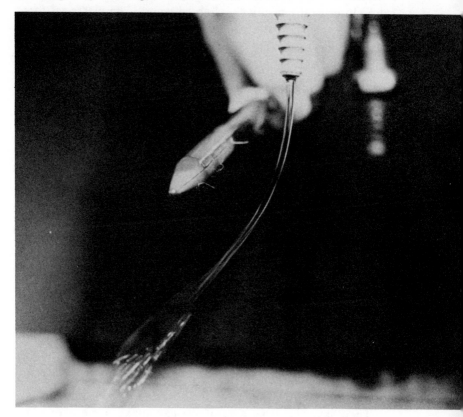

Explanation

Water molecules are dipolar. This means that while the overall charge on the molecules is neutral, one side of the molecules is slightly negative and the opposite side is slightly positive.

When you rub the "wand" with wool, it becomes charged. If the wand acquires a positive charge and you hold it near the falling water, the negative sides of the water molecules will be attracted by the positively charged wand and the positive sides of the molecules will be repelled. Therefore, the molecules will turn so that the negative sides of the molecules are closer to the positively charged wand. The electrical force between charges decreases as the distance between the charges increases. The water molecules have turned so that the negative ends are closer to the positively charged rod. Consequently, the attractive forces between the negative ends of the molecules and the positive wand will be larger than the repelling forces between the more distant positive ends of the molecules and the wand. The stream, therefore, will move toward the wand.

SCENE 23: FLOATING METAL AND THE MAGIC SINKING POWDER (for a small audience)

Action! Place a small boat made of aluminum foil on top of a large beaker of water. The boat floats. "Nothing mysterious about that," you say to the audience. "You all know that metal boats can float. They're hollow inside. But this boat will float even when it's full of holes!"

Pick up the boat and punch holes in its bottom with a pin. It still floats when placed on the water.

Then announce that you've invented a "magic powder" that makes even persistent boats such as this one sink. Sprinkle a pinch or two of the powder in the boat and it soon sinks.

Then say, "Now let's see if we can make a piece of non-boatlike metal float!"

With the help of a bent paper clip, place an unbent paper clip gently on the surface of another large beaker of water. It floats! To make it sink, add a pinch of your "magic powder" to the water.

Props and Prep

    2 large, clean beakers or containers
    2 paper clips
    Aluminum foil

Pin
Water
Cleaning or soap powder

Be sure the beakers and the water in them are both very clean. The "magic powder" is the cleaning or soap powder.

Explanation

Water molecules hold together so well that they form a surface that is skinlike. Just as your skin will bend and stretch when you push on it, so will the surface of clean water. Therefore, light objects such as aluminum foil, paper clips, razor blades, etc., even though denser than water, will not penetrate the "skin" if placed carefully on it. You can see that these objects really are more dense than water because once under the "skin," they sink.

Soap gets between the water molecules on the surface and

reduces the attractive forces between them. When this happens, the "skin" disappears.

SCENE 24: FUSED STREAMS (for a small audience)

Action! Place a large metal can of water on the edge of a table and a pail on the floor beneath it. Remove a piece of tape from the bottom of the can and three or four streams will emerge from holes punched in the can.

Now announce that you will squeeze the streams together. With your thumb and index finger, you "grasp" the outside streams and "squeeze" them inward. The streams fuse to form a single stream. After you remove your hand, the streams remain fused, as shown in the photograph.

Then flick your fingers outward from the center of the fused stream and they separate!

Props and Prep

> Large metal can
> Small nail
> Pail
> Tape
> Hammer
> Water
> Table

Use a hammer and a small nail to punch three or four holes about ½ centimeter ($\frac{3}{16}$ inch) apart near the bottom of the can. Cover the holes with tape and fill the can with water.

Explanation

Water molecules attract one another quite strongly. Once you bring the streams into contact with each other, they tend to stick together. If you overcome the attractive forces by separating the stream with your fingers, the streams will again flow along separate paths.

SCENE 25: OUT CANDLE!

Action! Announce to your audience that you are going to call upon the genie hidden in a large plastic container to put out the candle flame on a table several meters away. Lay the container on its side, with its open top aimed at the candle. Say to the container, "Now, genie!" Nothing happens. Grasp the container and hit it on its bottom with a mallet and shout, "Come on, genie—wake up!" The candle flame suddenly flickers and goes out.

Props and Prep

> 5 gallon plastic container with opening
>   in or near the center of the top

Mallet
Candle
Holder
Matches

Practice aiming and hitting the container a few times so you can extinguish the flame without fail.

Since a burning candle is used in this scene, you should **exercise the usual safety rules regarding open flames.**

Explanation

When you hit the container, the mallet drives the bottom of the container inward. This forces a sudden blast of air out the opening toward the flame. The moving air pushes the burning gases off the wick of the candle.

Act VII

More Magic
Through Chemistry

Many of the chemicals used in this act are not found around the house. You can probably find some of them in a chemistry set if you have one or in the chemical stock of a junior high or high school. Perhaps your science teacher will let you use some of these chemicals and encourage you to try some of the scenes in this act as a science project. You might even perform this act for your classmates after you have perfected it.

A few of the chemicals you will be using are poisonous. Be sure to follow directions carefully. **Use a chemical spatula or similar device for handling chemicals. Wash your hands and all glassware and other utensils thoroughly when you are finished.**

Because of the potential danger in these scenes, **all scenes in Act VII should be done under supervision of an adult!**

SCENE 1: A BURNING MESSAGE

Action! Touch a *glowing* (not flaming) splint to a plain sheet of white paper in two places. A message burns itself along the paper spelling out MAGIC SHOW, SCIENCE MAGIC, or whatever words you wish.

Props and Prep

Beaker or tumbler
Water
Potassium nitrate (KNO₃)
Small paintbrush (water-color type best)
2 sheets of white paper
Wooden splint (a thin piece of wood such as a coffee stirrer)
Matches
Chemical spatula
Scotch tape

In a beaker or tumbler prepare a saturated solution of potassium nitrate by dissolving as much of the solid as you can in 20 milliliters (⅔ ounce) of water.

Dip the small paintbrush in this solution and write an invisible message on a sheet of white paper. Trace the message several times to be sure you have enough of the compound on the paper. Write in such a way that the letters are connected; otherwise, the magic writing will stop between letters. Use a pencil to make small marks at the beginning of the first letter and at the end of the last. Tape this sheet of paper to an identical one and let it dry thoroughly.

To prepare a glowing splint, light a coffee stirrer or tongue depressor and let it burn for a few seconds. Then blow the flame out and blow on the ember to keep it glowing. Touch the glowing part to the first and last letters of the invisible ink and it will burn along the "writing" without igniting the paper.

Be sure there are no flammable objects nearby and that there is no danger of fire spreading if the paper should accidentally catch on fire. Observe all safety rules.

Explanation

When heated, potassium nitrate, which is one of the ingredients in gunpowder, decomposes. The oxygen this process produces enables other substances to burn. Once the paper on which the words are written begins to burn it, enough heat is supplied to continue the decomposition of the nitrate.

The paper not in contact with the nitrate doesn't burn. At the temperature of the reaction, there is enough oxygen for burning only where the nitrate is decomposing.

SCENE 2: A COPPER CHRISTMAS TREE

Action! Add about a gram ($\frac{1}{30}$ ounce) of white powder to a large beaker of water and stir to dissolve. Then hang a small sheet of copper, cut to look like an evergreen tree, in the solution.

Toward the end of the show, the tree will look like a snow-covered Christmas tree. Meanwhile, you can carry out your other scenes and return to this one after an hour or so.

Props and Prep

> Silver nitrate ($AgNO_3$) **(poisonous)**
> Beaker
> Water (distilled or rain water if possible)
> Thin sheet of copper
> Chemical spatula
> Scissors
> Thread

Use about 1 gram ($\frac{1}{30}$ ounce) of silver nitrate for every 250 milliliters ($7\frac{1}{2}$ ounces) of water. Unless you have very soft water, you will need to use distilled or rain water to dissolve the silver nitrate crystals. In hard water the crystals react with dissolved salts to form a cloudy white precipitate.

Do not touch the silver nitrate crystals or solution with your hands. It can burn your skin or eyes leaving small dark spots.

Cut the copper with scissors to look like a Christmas tree.

Punch a hole near the top of the tree so it can be suspended by a thread.

This scene might be a good way to start a Christmas show. By the end of the show, you could hold up the tree and wish everyone a Merry Christmas!

Explanation

Copper reacts with silver nitrate and forms silver metal and copper nitrate as the copper slowly dissolves. The silver crystals settle on the copper tree forming a beautiful snowlike cover. As the reaction goes on, the liquid takes on a bluish tint due to the copper. (You will find that most copper compounds form blue or bluish green solutions. If the solution were evaporated, silver metal and blue crystals of copper nitrate would remain.)

SCENE 3: THE PHILOSOPHERS' STONE

Action! Early in your program briefly discuss the history of alchemy and the search for the philosophers' stone that alchemists believed would enable them to change baser metals to gold. Mention that you have found a way to change iron to copper, but that the secret of converting substances to gold is still unknown.

Stand a shiny iron nail in a blue liquid and announce that the iron in the liquid will change to copper if left for a while.

Several scenes later, return to the nail. When you remove it from the liquid, the lower end of the nail has been changed to copper!

Then pick up a stone lying nearby and shout, "Eureka! I think it's the philosophers' stone!" Place the stone to your ear and listen. Then pour about 50 milliliters (1⅔ ounces) of a clear liquid into an equal volume of another. Stir the mixture and then rub the stone in your hand. Suddenly the liquid mixture turns to gold!

Props and Prep
   Copper sulfate ($CuSo_4 \cdot 5H_2O$) **(poisonous)**
   Sodium arsenite ($NaAsO_2$) **(poisonous)**
   Glacial acetic acid (CH_3COOH) **(poisonous)**
   Sodium thiosulfate ("hypo") ($Na_2S_2O_3$)
   Graduated cylinder
   3 beakers
   Chemical spatula
   Glass stirring rod
   Balance for weighing chemicals
   Stone
   Iron nail
   Steel wool
   Paper
   Water
   Soap or detergent

This is a very effective scene but it involves a number of **poisonous chemicals.** There is no danger if you are careful. **Keep all chemicals away from your hands and mouth.** Use paper and a spatula to transfer chemicals. **Wash all glassware and your hands thoroughly after you've made the solutions.**

To be on the safe side, ask an adult to help you with this scene if you are not thoroughly familiar with chemical techniques.

For the demonstration with the nail, prepare about 100 milliliters (3⅓ ounces) of a saturated solution of copper sulfate in a beaker. This requires about 50 grams (1⅔ ounces) of solid copper sulfate in 100 milliliters of soft, distilled, or rain water. Stir thoroughly; any excess solid can be left on the bottom of the beaker. Shine the nail with the steel wool. (Copper sulfate may be purchased in hardware stores.)

The solutions used to make the "gold" are prepared as follows:
Solution 1: Dissolve 1 gram (1/30 ounce) of sodium arsenite in 50 milliliters (1⅔ ounces) of water. Stir thoroughly. Then

add 5½ milliliters (1⅙ ounces) of glacial acetic acid. Stir.
Solution 2: Dissolve 10 grams (⅓ ounces) of sodium thiosulfate in 50 milliliters (1⅔ ounces) of water. Stir.

After the scene, pour the "gold" down the sink and flush it
away with lots of water. Rinse the beaker, with lots of water
too.

Explanation

When iron (Fe^0) is placed in a copper sulfate solution, the
iron dissolves and copper metal (Cu^0) comes out of solution.
(The ^{0} sign above the symbols for iron and copper indicate
that the atoms carry no electric charge.) At the atomic level
we believe that uncharged iron atoms give negatively charged
electrons to the positively charged copper ions (Cu^{++})
(charged atoms are called "ions") in solution. Thus the iron
atoms become positively charged ions (Fe^{++}) through this
process and dissolve, while copper ions become uncharged
atoms (Cu^0), which are not soluble. The reaction may be
thought of as taking place in the steps summarized by the
equations below.

$$\text{Step 1: } Fe^0 \longrightarrow Fe^{++} + 2 \text{ electrons}$$

$$\text{Step 2: } Cu^{++} + 2 \text{ electrons} \longrightarrow Cu^0$$

$$\text{Net Reaction: } Fe^0 + Cu^{++} \longrightarrow Fe^{++} + Cu^0$$

When the two solutions are mixed to make "gold," several
reactions take place. The first of these is quite slow. It involves the reaction between sodium thiosulfate and acetic acid
to form hydrogen sulfide gas. Once formed, this gas reacts
with the sodium arsenite to release the yellow precipitate—ar-
senic sulfide (As_2S_5). It is *not* gold!

SCENE 4: A STIRRED-UP REFRIGERATOR

Action! Fill a small beaker nearly to the top with a white
powder. Then sprinkle a few drops of water on top of small

wooden block. Place the beaker on top of the water drops. Pour water into the beaker until it is about three quarters full. Stir the mixture rapidly with a glass rod or stick while holding the rim of the beaker with your finger tips. After a minute or two lift the beaker. The block sticks to the beaker; they are frozen together. If the block is separated from the beaker, the audience can see the ice that has formed.

Props and Prep

Ammonium nitrate (NH_4NO_3) **(slightly poisonous)**
Small beaker
Small wooden block
Glass rod or stick
Water

The white powder added to the beaker is ammonium nitrate.

Explanation

When ammonium nitrate dissolves in water, heat is absorbed. The heat absorbed comes from the water so the temperature of the solution decreases. Stirring speeds up the dissolving process, causing heat to be rapidly absorbed and the temperature of the beaker quickly declines well below the freezing point of water ($0°$ C, $32°$ F). At this low temperature, the water drops in contact with the beaker lose heat to the colder beaker and freeze.

You might like to try this scene with a small thermometer that you could place in the solution to see how cold it becomes.

SCENE 5: A PAPER BATTERY (for a small audience)

Action! Place a sheet of copper on an old newspaper and attach one end of a clip-lead to the copper and the other end to one side of a bulb holder. Connect one end of a second

clip-lead to the other side of the bulb holder and the other end
to a sheet of zinc. Dip a folded paper towel into a beaker of
liquid and lay it over the copper. Then sprinkle a black
powder on the wet towel, place the zinc plate on top, and
gently press down on the "sandwich." The bulb in the bulb
holder lights and will continue to glow for some time.

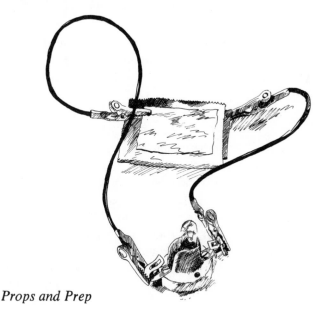

Props and Prep

Newspaper
Copper sheet (about 5 by 10 cm [2 by 4 inches])
Zinc sheet (same size as the copper sheet)
Bulb holder
2 clip-leads
GE ⚡48 bulb
Ammonium nitrate (NH_4NO_3)
Water
Beaker
Paper towel
Chemical spatula
Manganese dioxide (MnO_2) **(poisonous)**

The liquid into which the towel is dipped is a saturated solution of ammonium nitrate; to make this, dissolve as much ammonium nitrate as you can in 100 milliliters (3⅓ ounces) of water. The black powder sprinkled on the wet towel is manganese dioxide. The newspaper will protect the table top from becoming soiled by the dark maganese dioxide powder.

(You can use bulbs other than the GE ⅜48, but this bulb glows with very small currents and is, therefore, more reliable for this scene because the currents generated are quite small.)

Be sure to wash your hands after building this electric cell! Your hands may be somewhat soiled by the dark manganese dioxide powder.

Explanation

The cell you built operates much like the D cells used in flashlights. The zinc plate is the negative pole of the cell just as the zinc case of a D cell is the negative pole of the cell. The copper sheet is the positive pole, but you could use a carbon plate or rod like the ones found in D cells. (If you take a D cell apart, you will find a carbon rod in the center.) The moist towel soaked in ammonium nitrate allows ions (charged atoms) to move within your cell, while the black manganese dioxide prevents gas from collecting around the zinc electrode.

SCENE 6: DISAPPEARING GLASS

Action! Place a small Pyrex beaker into a larger Pyrex beaker and announce that you will make the small beaker disappear.

Pour a clear "magic" liquid into the smaller beaker. As the liquid rises around the smaller beaker, the lower portion of this vessel disappears. When the liquid level covers the small beaker, it disappears completely!

Props and Prep

    Pyrex beaker (250 or 400 ml [8 or 12 oz])
    Pyrex beaker (100 or 150 ml [3 or 4½ oz])
    Carbon tetrachloride (CCl$_4$) **(poisonous)**
    Benzene (C$_6$H$_6$) **(poisonous)**
    Large bottle for preparing and storing liquid
    Cork or cap for bottle
    Graduated cylinder
    Glass rod

In the mixing jar combine 300 milliliters (10 ounces) of carbon tetrachloride with 210 milliliters (7 ounces) of benzene. **Since both are poisonous, do not breathe their vapors or get them on your hands.** The liquids can best be poured into the beakers along a glass rod, as shown in the photograph. **While working with these liquids, keep the windows open.** Pour the mixture back into the bottle and seal it as soon as you complete the scene.

Explanation

When light passes from one substance to another, the light is bent (refracted). The amount the light bends is related to what is called the "optical density" (or index of refraction) of a substance. A vacuum has an optical density of 1.00. Air is about the same. Water is 1.33. Glass is 1.50. Diamond is 2.52. These numbers tell you that diamond bends light more than glass, which, in turn, bends light more than water. However, if two substances have the same index of refraction, light is not affected as it passes from one substance to the other. The mixture of benzene and carbon tetrachloride has the same index of refraction as Pyrex glass, so light passes through the submerged beaker as if the beaker were not there, and it becomes invisible to the viewer.

SCENE 7: ICE ON FIRE

Action! With a chemical spatula or forceps pick up a small chunk of solid material and place it on a piece of ice. After a few seconds, bring a burning match near the solid which now appears to be bubbling on the ice. A sputtering flame is produced. The ice is on fire!

Props and Prep

Calcium carbide (CaC_2) in small lumps **(poisonous)**
Shallow dish to hold ice

Chemical spatula or forceps
Ice cube
Matches

Calcium carbide can probably be obtained from a school laboratory.

The surface of the ice should be damp before you place a lump of calcium carbide on it. **Keep calcium carbide away from mouth and skin. Do not handle it with your fingers! Use a spatula or forceps! (Calcium carbide will react with the moisture on your skin and produce burns.)**

Keep the flames produced away from all flammable objects.

Explanation

Calcium carbide reacts with water (melted ice in this scene) to form the flammable gas acetylene (C_2H_2). The chemical equation for this reaction is:

$$CaC_2 + 2H_2O \longrightarrow Ca(OH)_2 + C_2H_2$$

calcium carbide + water $\longrightarrow$ calcium hydroxide + acetylene

It is, of course, the acetylene that's burning, not the ice. Because burning acetylene releases large amounts of heat, it is used in welding torches.

SCENE 8: EXPLODING BUBBLES

Action! Dip the end of a tube leading from a flask into a shallow dish of liquid. A bubble forms at the end of the tube. Shake the tube to release the bubble. Instead of falling, the bubble rises to the ceiling.

Your assistant lights a wooden splint while you prepare another bubble. You again shake the bubble free. As it rises toward the ceiling, your assistant touches it with the burning splint. The bubble suddenly explodes!

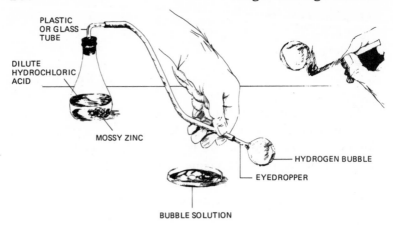

PLASTIC
OR GLASS
TUBE

DILUTE
HYDROCHLORIC
ACID

MOSSY ZINC

HYDROGEN BUBBLE

EYEDROPPER

BUBBLE SOLUTION

Props and Prep

Pyrex flask (125 or 250 ml [4 or 8 oz])
Stopper with 1 hole to fit flask
Glass or plastic tube to fit the hole in stopper
Rubber tubing
Eyedropper
Dilute hydrochloric (muriatic) acid (HCl) **(poisonous)**
Mossy zinc
Soap solution (sold in toy stores; or use a solution of dish-
    washing soap or detergent)
Shallow dish
Thin wooden splints or long fireplace matches
Safety glasses

Ask a science teacher for some dilute hydrochloric acid
(one part acid added to two parts water; **never add water to
acid). Do not attempt to prepare this acid yourself!**

While doing this scene **wear safety glasses to protect your
eyes in case the acid should accidentally spill or splatter.**

**If acid gets on your skin, quickly wash it away with plenty of
cold water. If it should spill on the floor, pour baking soda on
it.**

To generate hydrogen, pour about 50 milliliters (1⅔

ounces) of acid into the flask and add a few pieces of mossy zinc.

One end of the rubber tube is connected to the glass tube that passes through the stopper in the flask. In the other end insert the narrow end of an eyedropper from which the bulb has been removed.

To make the bubbles, dip the *wide end* of the eyedropper into the bubble solution. The hydrogen gas will inflate the bubble. Gently jiggle the rubber tube to detach the bubble from the eyedropper.

Ignite the free bubbles well away from and above the flask and the eyedropper. Hydrogen is flammable! If a flame were to reach the flask, it might explode, so be very careful in doing this scene. Be sure there are no flammable objects nearby when you try it. Observe all safety rules regarding use of flames.

Explanation

Hydrogen gas is much less dense than air so the gas-filled bubbles rise. However, if the bubbles are small, they will sink in air. (Do you know why? Remember—part of a bubble is a liquid!)

When hydrogen burns, water is formed. The chemical equation that summarizes the reaction is given below:

$$2H_2 + O_2 \longrightarrow 2H_2O$$

hydrogen + oxygen $\longrightarrow$ water

Since the bubbles contain hydrogen, they will combine with the oxygen in air if ignited. If the bubbles contain pure hydrogen, the gas burns from the surface inward quite quickly but quietly. If air is mixed with the hydrogen, the reaction occurs throughout the bubble so the burning is very rapid and explosive! The first few bubbles produced will contain air as well as hydrogen because the flask, of course, contained air at the start.

Act VIII

Colored Chemical Magic

The scenes in Act VIII are probably the most dramatic ones described in this book. However, most of the chemicals you will need can be obtained only from a school's chemical supply shelves. Ask a science teacher if you may have some of these chemicals. Perhaps your science teacher will let you do some of the scenes in this act as a science project. It would certainly make an exciting show to present to your science classmates.

Warning: Many of the chemicals used in this act are **poisonous** so you will have to **work very carefully!** Follow all the safety rules you read about in "Before the Show Begins."

Wash your hands thoroughly after preparing chemical solutions and again following the clean-up after the scenes.

Rinse all vessels thoroughly with water after you are through with them. Then wash them with soap and hot water.

All scenes in Act VIII should be done under adult supervision.

SCENE 1: A BLUE MESSAGE

Action! Show the audience a piece of white paper and say, "Let's see if the spirits have left us a message."

You move the paper back and forth above a flame. A message written in blue ink appears on the paper. It might say WELCOME TO *Magic,* WE'RE WITH YOU TODAY, DON'T BELIEVE IT, or whatever you wish.

After a few minutes, the message fades away.

Props and Prep

> Cobalt chloride ($CoCl_2 \cdot 6H_2O$) **(poisonous)**
> Small glass beaker or jar
> Graduated cylinder
> Water
> Small paintbrush (water-color type)
> Sheet of white paper
> Chemical spatula
> Alcohol or gas flame

Before the scene begins, prepare a saturated solution of cobalt chloride by dissolving as much cobalt chloride as possible in 100 milliliters (3⅓ ounces) of water. Use it as the "ink" to write your message on the sheet of paper with a small brush. When the "ink" dries, the cobalt chloride remains in the form of fine pink crystals, but the message will be nearly invisible.

Wash your hands thoroughly after this scene.

Explanation

Heating the paper will cause the faint pink crystals of cobalt chloride to decompose, forming anhydrous blue crystals.

As the blue crystals cool, they will recombine with moisture in the air and fade back to the nearly invisible pink crystals.

SCENE 2: A SOMETIMES BLUE BOTTLE

Action! Pick up a clear glass flask three quarters full of a cloudy solution. Say to the audience, "That's funny! This bottle used to blue." Shake the flask, keeping your hand over its stopper so it won't come out of the mouth of the flask. The flask turns blue!

Nod and say, "That's better! I knew it used to be blue."

Gradually, the blue color disappears; it will return when you shake the flask again.

You can continue to turn the color back to blue by shaking the bottle periodically throughout the performance.

Props and Prep

> Potassium hydroxide (KOH) **(poisonous)**
> Water
> Dextrose
> Methylene blue
> Glass flask (500 ml [17 oz], preferably round with flat base)
> Graduated cylinder
> Cork or stopper to fit flask
> Balance

Dissolve about 2½ grams (about $\frac{1}{10}$ ounce) of potassium hydroxide in about 500 milliliters (17 ounces) of water. **(Potassium hydroxide is a poisonous substance much like lye. Keep it off your skin.)** When this solution has cooled, add 1½ grams (about $\frac{1}{20}$ ounce) of dextrose and a pinch of methylene blue and swirl. Pour off about one quarter of the liquid and insert a stopper. After several days the solution turns a brownish yellow so you will have to prepare a fresh solution each time you do the show.

Explanation

In a basic solution (see Scene 6, "Explanation," below), methylene blue, which is a blue dye, is changed to a cloudy gray compound. When mixed with the oxygen in air, the gray compound is oxidized back to methylene blue. A clue to this action is the fact that the surface of the solution which is in contact with air will remain blue, while the materials within the liquid are gray.

SCENE 3: DELAYED DARK-BLUE MAGIC

Action! Pour equal volumes of two clear solutions labeled I and II into a glass beaker or tumbler. Tell your audience to watch closely. Say some "magic" words and snap your fingers. The clear mixture of liquids in the beaker *suddenly* turns dark blue!

Props and Prep

Potassium iodate (KIO_3)
Sodium bisulfite ($NaHSO_3$) **(slightly poisonous)**
Soluble starch
Saucepan
3 glass beakers or tumblers (250 ml [8 oz])
2 bottles (1 liter [1 qt] for storing) with stoppers
Solutions I and II (see below)
Graduated cylinder
Balance
Heat source (stove, burner, hot plate)
Watch with second hand
Water

Prepare two solutions, I and II, as described below. Store them in labeled tightly stoppered bottles.

SOLUTION I: Dissolve 15 grams (½ ounce) of potassium iodate in 1 liter (1 quart) of water.

SOLUTION II: Dissolve 4 grams (⅐ ounce) of soluble starch in 500 milliliters (16 ounces) of boiling water. When the starch has dissolved, add 15 grams (½ ounce) of sodium bisulfite and another 500 milliliters of water.

You can keep Solutions I and II for months. Before the act begins, dilute Solution II (or both, if you prefer) with water until you have a satisfactory time delay (5 to 10 seconds is good) between the mixing of the two solutions and the sudden appearance of the dark color.

Be sure to wash thoroughly all the glassware after use in this scene. One of the products is iodine which is very poisonous.

Explanation

This chemical reaction is often called the "iodine clock reaction." The dark color of the product is caused by iodine, which is present in the potassium iodate (KIO_3) in Solution I. The iodine reacts with the starch in Solution II to form a complex dark blue chemical.

The reactions that take place before the iodine is produced are quite slow. The time these reactions take, are related to the concentration of the reacting substances. You can carry out experiments to see this for yourself by mixing the solutions at various dilutions. For instance, you might measure the time it takes after mixing for undiluted solutions to react and turn blue and compare that with the times taken using the dilutions with water in the following table:

Solution I dilution	*Solution II dilution*
undiluted	undiluted
1:1	undiluted
1:2	undiluted
1:4	undiluted
1:1	1:1
1:1	1:2
1:1	1:4
etc.	

SCENE 4: COLORS FOR A HALLOWEEN HOLIDAY

Action! Three beakers of liquid are on the table. Each beaker contains 50 milliliters (1⅔ ounces) of liquid. The first beaker holds a liquid labeled Solution I, the second a liquid labeled Solution II, the third a liquid labeled Solution III. Pour the liquid labeled II into the liquid labeled III, then add the liquid labeled I to the mixture of liquids II and III. Swirl or stir to mix the liquids thoroughly. Suddenly the clear mixture turns *orange!* As you hold it up before your audience and say, "Look at the orange juice I have made," it just as suddenly turns to a dark blue color!

Props and Prep

Mercuric chloride ($HgCl_2$) **(poisonous)**
3 glass beakers or tumblers (250 ml [8 oz])
Balance
Graduated cylinder
Large stoppered bottle (1 liter [1 qt])
Solution I (see Scene 3)
Solution II (see Scene 3)
Water

To make Solution III, dissolve 3 grams ($\frac{1}{10}$ ounce) of mercuric chloride in 1 liter (1 quart) of water. Store in a tightly stoppered bottle. **Mercuric chloride is very poisonous. Keep it away from your skin and mouth.**

To increase the speed of the reaction, use less of Solution III.

Of course, you should **never let anyone drink the "orange juice." It is poisonous. So is the dark liquid.**

Explanation

This reaction is similar to the one in Scene 3. However, in this scene a series of slow reactions produce an orange precipitate before iodine is produced. Once the iodine forms, it reacts with the starch in Solution I to form a complex dark blue chemical.

SCENE 5: COLOR ON, COLOR OFF

Action! Add a drop of a clear "magic" solution to a beaker that is half full of another solution. The mixture becomes light red when stirred. Additional drops cause the red color to deepen.

Point out to your audience that just as a rheostat can be used to make a light bulb brighter, so drops of this "magic" liquid can be used to make a solution redder.

But a rheostat can be used to make a light dimmer too. Then ask your audience, "Can the deep red solution be made lighter?" As you ask this question, pick up a small crystal with forceps and add it to the deep red liquid. Stir the mixture and it becomes noticeably lighter. When more crystals are added, the solution lightens even more.

Drops of the first clear solution can be used to redden the solution again!

Props and Prep

  Potassium thiocyanate (KSCN) **(poisonous)**
  Ferric nitrate (Fe[NO₃]₃•9H₂O) **(poisonous)**
  Disodium hydrogen phosphate (Na₂HPO₄) (sometimes labeled dibasic sodium phosphate)
  Eyedropper
  Beakers or tumblers
  Glass stirring rod
  Graduated cylinder
  Forceps or chemical spatula
  Balance
  Water

Prepare a solution of potassium thiocyanate by adding 0.2 grams (0.007 ounces) of the crystals to 1 liter (1 quart) of water. Half fill a beaker with this solution.

Prepare a ferric nitrate solution by adding 10 grams (⅓ ounce) of the solid to 125 milliliters (4 ounces) of water. This is added to the potassium thiocyanate with an eyedropper. These chemicals are not highly poisonous, but you should avoid handling them with your fingers. **Wash your hands thoroughly after working with them.**

Explanation

The crystals added to the mixture to lighten the red color are disodium hydrogen phosphate.

When drops of ferric nitrate solution are added to the half-filled beaker containing potassium thiocyanate solution, the mixture turns red. The ferric ions (Fe^{+++}) affect the equilibrium that exists within the solution. The equilibrium is indicated by the double arrows in the drawing below.

$$Fe^{+++} + SCN^- \rightleftharpoons Fe\,SCN^{++}$$

ferric ion + thiocyanate ion $\rightleftharpoons$ (red) ferric thiocyanate ion

When the concentration of ferric ions increases, there are more collisions between ferric and thiocyanate ions. This results in the formation of more $FeSCN^{++}$ ions, which are red.

Adding crystals of disodium hydrogen phosphate removes ferric ions from the equilibrium by forming $FeHPO_4^+$ ions, which are colorless. With fewer ferric ions, the collisions between Fe^{+++} and SCN^- ions decrease. Thus the rate of formation of $FeSCN^{++}$ is reduced, while its rate of decomposition to Fe^{+++} and SCN^- remains the same. This causes the concentration of the red $FeSCN^{++}$ ions to decrease.

SCENE 6: RED, WHITE AND BLUE

Action! Sing (or say) to the audience, "Three cheers for the red . . . white . . . and blue!" As you sing these words, pour some clear liquid into each of three clear glasses. As you sing "red," the liquid poured into the first glass turns red. Similarly, as you sing "white," the liquid poured into the second glass turns white. As you sing "blue," liquid poured into the third glass turns blue.

Props and Prep

    Household ammonia (NH_3) **(poisonous)**
    3 clear glass tumblers or beakers
    Phenolphthalein solution **(poisonous)**
    Ethanol **(poisonous)**
    Water
    Mixing jar
    Lead acetate ($Pb[C_2H_3O_2]_2$) **(poisonous)**
    Copper sulfate hydrate ($CuSO_4 \cdot 6H_2O$) **(poisonous)**
    Chemical spatula
    Glass stirring rod

To make the phenolphthalein solution, add a gram (0.03 ounce) of phenolphthalein to a mixture of 50 milliliters (1⅔ ounces) of ethanol and 50 milliliters of water in a glass jar.

Pour a few drops of phenolphthalein solution in the first glass. Cover the bottom of the second glass with some lead acetate crystals. Cover the bottom of the third glass with copper sulfate hydrate crystals.

Again, these chemicals are poisonous. Handle the crystals with a chemical spatula. Wash your hands after preparing for the scene and after cleaning up.

Explanation:

(1) Phenolphthalein is an acid–base indicator that turns red in a basic solution. Since ammonia in water is basic, the phenolphthalein turns *red* when the ammonia is added.

A basic solution contains hydroxide ions (OH^-). An ammonia solution is basic because it reacts with water to form OH^- ions as shown in the equation below.

$$NH_3 + H_2O \rightleftharpoons NH_4^+ + OH^-$$

ammonia + water ⇌ ammonium ion + hydroxide ion

(2) When the lead ions in lead acetate come in contact

with the hydroxide ions in the ammonia solution, they combine to form the *white* insoluble compound—lead hydroxide ($Pb[OH]_2$).

$$Pb + 2OH^- \longrightarrow Pb(OH)_2 \downarrow$$

lead + hydroxide ions $\longrightarrow$ lead hydroxide

(3) The copper ions in copper sulfate react with ammonia to form a complex ion that has a deep *blue* color.

$$Cu^{++} + 4NH_3 \rightleftharpoons Cu(NH_3)_4^{++}$$

copper ion + ammonia $\rightleftharpoons$ (deep blue) copper ammonia complex ion

SCENE 7: A ROW OF COLORS

Action! Take a large beaker or pitcher containing a light blue solution and pour a small amount of it into the first of nine small beakers or tumblers lined up on a table. Swirl the small beaker and the liquid you have poured turns black.

Proceed to pour about the same volume of the light blue liquid into each of the other eight small vessels. Each time, swirl the vessel after pouring the liquid. The liquid in the eight other vessels become, respectively, dark blue, orange-brown, olive green, dark red-brown, yellow-green, bluish white, gray-green, and emerald green!

Props and Prep

Copper sulfate ($CuSO_4 \cdot 5H_2O$) **(poisonous)**
Distilled or rain water
Sodium sulfide (Na_2S) **(poisonous)**
Household ammonia (NH_3) **(poisonous)**
Potassium chromate (K_2CrO_4) **(poisonous)**
Potassium ferrocyanide ($K_4Fe[CN]_6$)
Potassium ferricyanide ($K_3Fe[CN]_6$)

Potassium carbonate K₂CO₃) **(poisonous)**

Potassium thiocyanate (KSCN) **(poisonous)**

Sodium bisulfite (NaHSO₃)

9 small glass beakers or tumblers (150 to 200 ml [5 to 7 oz])

Large beaker or pitcher

Chemical spatula

Eyedropper

Many of these chemicals are poisonous. Handle solids only with a chemical spatula. Wash your hands and all glassware thoroughly after doing this scene.

Dissolve in the large beaker or pitcher about 2 teaspoonsful of copper sulfate crystals in 1 liter (1 quart) of water. If the solution is cloudy, filter it. Use distilled or rain water if possible.

Place the nine small vessels in a row and add ahead of time the following materials:

Beaker	Add to empty beaker	Color after copper sulfate solution is added
1	A few crystals of sodium sulfide	black
2	A few drops of household ammonia	dark blue
3	A few crystals of potassium chromate	orange-brown
4	A few crystals of potassium chromate and a few drops of ammonia	olive green
5	A few crystals of potassium ferrocyanide	dark red-brown
6	A few crystals of potassium ferricyanide	yellow-green
7	A few crystals of potassium carbonate	bluish white
8	A very few crystals of potassium thiocyanate	gray-green

| 9 | A few crystals of sodium bisulfite | emerald green |

The solution you add to each beaker in order in this scene is copper sulfate.

Explanation

The copper sulfate solution reacts with each of the chemicals to form other chemicals that are different colors. For example, the addition of the solution to sodium sulfide produces a black precipitate that is copper sulfide (CuS). When the solution is added to ammonia, the copper ions (Cu^{++}) react to form complex ions of copper and ammonia ($Cu[NH_3]_4^{++}$), which are deep blue.

SCENE 8: SPRAY A FLAG

Action! Announce to your audience that you have discovered a secret formula that enables you to dissolve and then reassemble the American flag. Explain that the dissolved flag is in the liquid that fills an atomizer or spray bottle that you hold in your hand.

Then gently and evenly spray the liquid over a sheet of white paper tacked to the wall or lying on the table. The American flag appears on the paper!

Props and Prep

Potassium thiocyanate (KSCN) **(poisonous)**
Potassium ferrocyanide ($K_4Fe[CN]_6$)
Ferric chloride ($FeCl_3$) **(poisonous)**
3 glass beakers or tumblers
Atomizer or spray bottle (the kind used to spray window-washing liquid)
Small paintbrush (water-color type)
White paper, preferably lined
Water
Graduated cylinder
Teaspoon

Prepare a solution of potassium thiocyanate by dissolving a few of the crystals in 100 milliliters (3⅓ ounces) of water.

Prepare a solution of potassium ferrocyanide by dissolving about ½ teaspoonful of potassium ferrocyanide in 100 milliliters of water.

Prepare a solution of ferric chloride by dissolving about a teaspoonful of ferric chloride in 200 milliliters (6⅔ ounces) of water. Pour this last solution into atomizer or spray bottle.

Paint the flag on the white paper beforehand. Lined paper will help you to paint the stripes. The white stripes and stars will simply be the result of the unpainted paper. Paint the stripes that are to be red with the potassium thiocyanate solution. Rinse the brush and then paint the blue field with the potassium ferrocyanide solution. Both solutions are colorless.

Let the paper dry thoroughly before you perform this scene, when you spray it with the ferric chloride solution.

Again, some of these chemicals are poisonous. Don't touch them or bring them near your mouth. Wash all vessels thoroughly when you are finished.

Explanation

When the dry paper is sprayed, the potassium thiocyanate reacts with the ferric chloride mist to form ferric thiocyanate, a red compound. The potassium ferrocyanide combines with ferric chloride to form ferric ferrocyanide, a deep blue compound.

SCENE 9: HOT COLOR, COLD COLOR (for a small audience)

Action! Place a few small reddish crystals into a dry Pyrex test tube. Turn the tube so it is nearly horizontal and spread the red crystals out along the tube by gently tapping the tube.

Announce to your audience that you will change the color of these crystals. Using a test-tube holder, begin heating the tube over an alcohol burner or gas flame. The reddish crystals take on a deep-blue color.

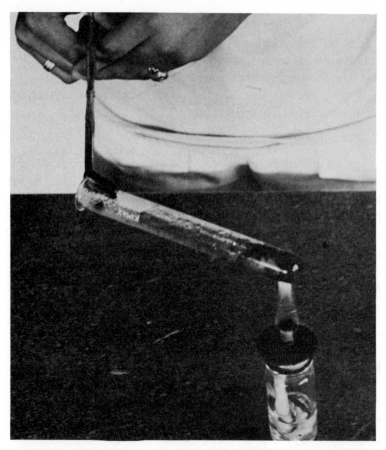

Then say that really you prefer red. Remove the tube from the flame and place it upright in a tumbler or beaker filled with ice water. The crystals slowly change from blue back to red!

Props and Prep

Cobalt chloride hydrate ($CoCl_2 \cdot 6H_2O$) **(poisonous)**
Pyrex test tube
Alcohol or gas burner
Test-tube holder
Beaker or glass
Ice
Water

The reddish crystals in the tube are cobalt chloride. **Keep cobalt chloride away from your skin. Wash your hands and the test tube thoroughly when you finish.**

If the air is very dry, add a drop of water to the crystals to change them back to red.

Explanation

Cobalt chloride combined with water forms a red hydrated salt. When heated, water is driven from the crystals to form blue dehydrated cobalt chloride. Upon cooling, the crystals recombine with moisture in the air and turn red again. (As noted above, if the air is very dry, you may have to increase the humidity in the tube by adding a drop of water.)

SCENE 10: COLORED ELECTRICAL WRITING

Action! Pick up a glass rod to which a pair of short, heavy copper wires are taped. Use two clip-leads to connect one of the wires to the positive pole of a 6- or 12-volt battery or battery charger and the other wire to the negative pole.

Dip a piece of filter paper in a white liquid and place it on a newspaper on a table. Then announce to your audience that you will write on the filter paper with electricity. As you move the double-tipped "pen" slowly along the paper, red and dark-blue lines appear side by side. The wire connected to the positive pole of the battery produces the dark-blue line, the wire connected to the negative pole produces the red line. (In the photograph the faint line is the red one.)

Props and Prep

   Heavy copper wire (#16 gauge)
   2 insulated wire clip-leads
   Glass rod or tube
   6- or 12-volt battery or battery charger
   Tape
   Sodium iodide (NaI)
   Cornstarch

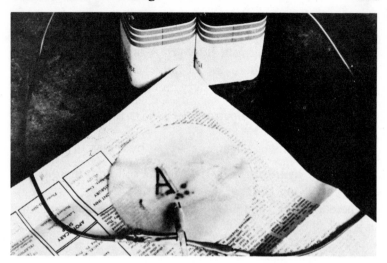

Phenolphtalein solution **(poisonous)**
Glass beaker or tumbler
Filter paper
Tablespoon
Balance
Newspaper
Water
Eyedropper
Stirrer

The filter paper is dipped in a mixture that you have prepared beforehand. It consists of 1 tablespoonful of corn-starch, 1 tablespoonful of sodium iodide, about 200 milliliters (6 ounces) of water, and about 2 eyedropperfuls of phenol-phthalein solution (see Scene 6, above). Stir the mixture to dissolve the iodide and suspend the starch. The starch will set-tle so you have to stir the mixture again just before you dip the filter paper into it.

Explanation

If you look carefully, you will see tiny gas bubbles coming from the negative electrode (the free end of the copper wire connected to the negative pole of the battery). This gas is hydrogen. Electrolysis is taking place in the moist area around both electrodes. Hydrogen ions (H^+) are positively charged so they are attracted to the negative electrode. There they pick up electrons from the battery and become hydrogen gas.

$$2H^+ + 2 \text{ electrons} \longrightarrow H_2 \text{ (gas)}$$

hydrogen ions + 2 electrons $\longrightarrow$ hydrogen (gas)

For every hydrogen ion (H^+) in the solution, there is also an hydroxide ion (OH^-).

These ions (H^+ and OH^-) come from the slight ionization of water.

$$H_2O \rightleftarrows H^+ + OH^-$$

water $\rightleftarrows$ hydrogen ion + hydroxide ion

As the H^+ ions are removed, the area around the negative electrode has more OH^- ions than H^+ ions. Because this region has an excess of OH^- ions, the solution is basic. As you remember from earlier scenes, phenolphthalein is red in a basic solution, so the area near the negative electrode turns red.

At the positive electrode, iodide ions (I^-) release electrons (that flow to the battery) and become neutral iodine molecules.

$$2I^- \longrightarrow I_2 + 2 \text{ electrons}$$

iodine ions $\longrightarrow$ iodine + 2 electrons

Because there are starch particles on the paper, the iodine reacts with the starch to form complex molecules that have a dark-blue color. Thus the area around the positive electrode turns dark blue.

ROBERT GARDNER was a staff member of the Elementary Science Study and the Physical Science Group at the Education Development Center in Newton, Massachusetts, for a period of three years while on leave from the Salisbury School, Salisbury, Connecticut, where he currently teaches physics, chemistry, and physical science and is Chairman of the Science Department as well as Director of Admissions of the Summer School. He has written several science books for children, including *Shadow Science* (Doubleday, 1976), and numerous articles for *Nature and Science, The Science Teacher, The Biology Teacher, The Physics Teacher, Science and Children,* and *Current Science.*

S